PERFECT DARK ™

Prima's Official Strategy Guide

Tri Pham
Jeff Barton
Mario De Govia
Kevin Sakamoto
Brandon Smith
Donato Tica

Prima Games
A Division of Prima
Communications, Inc.

3000 Lava Ridge Court
Roseville, CA 95661
(916) 787-7000
www.primagames.com

The Prima Games logo is a trademark of Prima Communications, Inc. Prima Publishing® is a registered trademark of Prima Communications, Inc., registered in the U.S. Patent and Trademark Office.

© 2000 by Prima Publishing. All rights reserved. No part of this book may be reproduced or transmitted in any form or by any means, electronic or mechanical, including photocopying, recording, or by any information storage or retrieval system without written permission from Prima Publishing, except for the inclusion of quotations in a review.

Senior Editor/Additional Text: Richard Dal Porto
Assistant Project Editor: Candace English
Senior Product Manager: Sara E. Wilson
Senior Designer: Kari Keating

©2000 Nintendo. Game by Rare. Perfect Dark ™ and © 2000 Rare. The Rareware logo is a trademark of Rare.

All products and characters mentioned in this book are trademarks of their respective companies.

Acknowledgements

Prima Games and the Creative Development Department would like to thank Rare for creating such an awesome game. We would also like to thank the following people at Nintendo: Jennifer Loftus, Tom Hertzog, and Dougall Campbell for their help and patience. Tony Myhre, Luke Rowan, and Jolanda Ledoux for putting up with us. At Prima: Sara Wilson, Pan Lee, Richard Dal Porto, and Candace English for their support. Much props go to Stacey for the wonderful weekend, Anne for the three-week loan, Justin for holding the fort, Emily for her love, Grandma Sakamoto for her strength, Greg and Kari for the looks, and Uwajimaya for the hopia, ube, and the Super Colas.

Important:
Prima Publishing has made every effort to determine that the information contained in this book is accurate. However, the publisher makes no warranty, either expressed or implied, as to the accuracy, effectiveness, or completeness of the material in this book; nor does the publisher assume liability for damages, either incidental or consequential, that may result from using the information in this book. The publisher cannot provide information regarding gameplay, hints and strategies, or problems with hardware or software. Questions should be directed to the support numbers provided by the game and device manufacturers in their documentation. Some game tricks require precise timing and may require repeated attempts before the desired result is achieved.

ISBN: 7615-2280-8
Library of Congress Catalog Card Number: 99-63698
Printed in the United States of America

00 01 02 03 GG 10 9 8 7 6 5 4 3 2 1

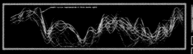

contents

Game Basics

PERFECT DARK™

The Story

Your name is Joanna Dark. You've just finished training at the Carrington Institute and are ready for your first assignment. They code named you Perfect Dark at the Institute because of your incredible skills. That's why you've been selected for this highly dangerous and sensitive mission.

Daniel Carrington, your boss and head of the CI, believes that a firm called dataDyne Corporation is involved with shady extraterrestrial activities. These suspicions were recently confirmed when CI received a distress signal from a Dr. Caroll. Apparently, he is being held against his will to perform experiments deep within dataDyne Headquarters.

Your first mission is to retrieve this Dr. Caroll from dataDyne HQ. The information he carries could be vital to the survival of the human race. Are you ready?

The Basics

Difficulty Levels

The solo missions in *Perfect Dark* can be played in three difficulty levels: Agent, Special Agent, and Perfect Agent. Once you complete the game as a Perfect Agent, you open up a fourth mode, Perfect Dark.

AGENT//Perfect for beginners, Agent mode is very forgiving. The opponents are weak and have poor aim. This mode allows the player to get familiar with the controls and practice the basic techniques. The objectives are few and generally straightforward.

In Agent mode, the first mission has only one objective. Simple enough, isn't it?

SPECIAL AGENT//So you've proven yourself as an Agent. But do you have what it takes to be a Special Agent? Your enemies are a little smarter and tougher. In addition, they've improved their aim a little too. Hopefully, you've learned the maps as an Agent, because there are more objectives to complete in this mode. This means that areas may now be open that were previously closed to you.

More skills, more objectives. This is the same mission as above, but with more objectives.

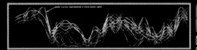

PERFECT AGENT//
You think you've got what it takes? Here's your chance to prove it. The enemies here rarely miss and their shots sting a little more. They are also better shielded. As if that weren't enough, you're usually provided with less ammo than in the other modes. With a full load of objectives, you'd better know your maps.

Even more objectives? Only a Perfect Agent can accomplish these lofty goals and survive to tell about it.

PERFECT DARK//
Once you've completed the solo missions as a Perfect Agent, Perfect Dark mode is unlocked. The objectives are the same as they are in Perfect Agent. The difference here is that you are allowed to change your enemies' health, accuracy, and damage.

Now that you've earned your stars, you can tweak to your heart's content.

Co-Operative Mode

Two are better than one.

In this mode, you get to team up with one of your buddies or up to four Simulants. Using a split screen, you and your partner set out to complete the mission together. Charge into a room full of baddies together and wreck shop. Or, if you prefer, split up to complete different objectives. Check the solo mission walkthrough for tips on where and when to do which.

Counter-Operative Mode

Sometimes it's more fun to be the bad guy.

In Counter-Operative mode, you and a friend square off in the now familiar solo mission Scenarios. One player runs through and tries to complete the objectives while the second player, as the Counter-Operative, tries to stop him. If the Counter-Operative is taken out, he is immediately transferred into another body to continue the chase.

PERFECT DARK™

General Strategies

To be a Perfect Agent, you're going to need some mad skills. Just knowing the following techniques isn't going to be enough. You need to instinctively know when and how to use them. Study them well.

STRAFING//Also called sidestepping, strafing is the very foundation of first-person shooters. Using the default control scheme, use ©◄ and ©► to move side to side.

Strafe when fighting an opponent head-to-head. You'll keep your enemies in view at all times and your weapon aimed in their direction while making it harder for them to hit you.

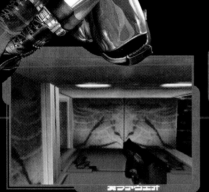

Strafe around corners to avoid being blindsided. As you're approaching a corner to make a left turn, start turning before you actually reach the corner. At the same time, begin to strafe right. This allows you to immediately see what's down the next hallway while keeping your back to the wall.

RELOADING//There's nothing worse than having your target lined up, only to find when you pull the trigger that your clip is empty. Because it takes a moment to reload, no matter what weapon you're using, it's important to do it at the right times. Follow these simple but crucial tips and you'll never get caught with your pants down.

— When you need to reload, take cover if possible.

— Keep an eye on your ammo indicator. Reloading a little early is better than a little late.

— Never run around with an empty clip. The best time to reload is when no enemies are present.

— In multiplayer showdowns, be aware of your opponents' reloading pattern. If you know when *they're* going to reload, *you* can safely reload. Better yet, take advantage of their vulnerable moment and fire a few rounds into them.

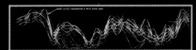

AIMING//For obvious reasons, aiming is key. A few techniques can improve your success rate.

— Call up your sights by holding Ⓡ. This ensures that you have your target lined up. Be careful when you do this. You can't move while your sights are up.

— For steady aim, use Ⓒ to line up your shot. This only works if you're in a safe place or if your target can't see you. This is steadier than using Ⓡ because you're not holding onto the Control Stick.

— If you're confused as to which target is an enemy and which is friendly, call up your sights and the color of the box will change: blue for friendly, red for hostile.

QUICK STEP//The Quick Step requires a wall or some obstacle that you can use for cover.

Stand near the edge of the wall and facing it.

Holding Ⓡ, press Ⓒ◄ or Ⓒ► to peek out.

This shoot-and-hide technique is the safest way to deal with tough enemies. Stay behind the cover until your opponents' gunfire has stopped. Then, peek out and pepper them with your own gunfire. This technique is especially useful for destroying security cameras and turret guns. Don't forget to reload while behind cover.

DOORS//The doors allow for a couple of useful fighting techniques.

Shoot through the glass windows on the doors for some undetected kills.

Engage your enemy behind an open door. Unload on them while the door is open. Close the door if they begin to shoot back or if you need to reload.

Co-Operative Strategies

WITH SIMULANTS//Playing the Co-Operative missions with Simulants is pretty straightforward. Throw them in the mix and they'll simply help you gun down your enemies. The one thing you have to watch out for is their lack of tact. Use the Quick menu and press Z until you come to the Simulants menu. Simulant buddies have three commands: Passive, Aggressive, and Stealth. In areas where stealth is key, they can sometimes give you away. Use Stealth to have your Sim buddy disappear for five seconds of sneaking around without them.

WITH A BUDDY//Sharing your missions with a friend can be a little more interesting. Here are a few tips to keep things smooth.

— In heavily guarded areas, stay close to each other and gang up on the enemies.

— Watch each other's back so enemies can't sneak up on you.

— Divide up the targets. For instance, have one player target only opponents on the left side of the room, and the other on the right side. This prevents shooting at already dead targets.

— Split up in lightly guarded areas to accomplish multiple objectives at once.

— Decide ahead of time what each player's duties will be. Don't get caught arguing about who gets to do what while an army of guards comes charging at you.

— In areas and missions with key cards, the players must stay together. Otherwise, the one without a card will be locked out and left behind.

CHARACTERS

PROFILE

Highly trained but inexperienced, she has superb reactions and is proficient with a variety of weapons—a very competent all-around agent. Her training scores—the highest recorded—resulted in the creation of a new class of training grade. Because she's the embodiment of the Carrington Institute's ideal agent, her code name is "Perfect Dark."

CI File #027

Training Status:	Complete
Training Grade:	A++
Active Status:	Assigned

Age: 23 years 2 months
Race: Human (Female)

Joanna Dark

Jonathan

PROFILE

Our most experienced undercover agent, he's highly accurate with his chosen weapon (a Magnum Revolver). He's perfectly suited to undercover missions, but less suited to out-and-out combat. Before Joanna Dark, he held the highest recorded training scores.

CI File #009

Training Status:	Complete
Training Grade:	A+
Active Status:	Undercover

Age: 28 years 5 months
Race: Human (Male)

Daniel Carrington

PROFILE

An intelligent patriarchal scientist/entrepreneur, and the founder of the Carrington Institute, he plans all missions carried out by his agents and runs each operation direct from a link in his office. He has strange taste in clothes.

Age: 62 years 8 months
Race: Human (Male)

Analyst Note

The head of dataDyne Corp., she is addicted to power and dislikes being anybody's underling. She hates it when she loses the initiative, and she's prepared to do extremely unscrupulous things to get ahead of her competition—especially Daniel Carrington, whom she loathes.

Cassandra de Vries

Age: 39 years 7 months
Race: Human (Female)

■ ■ ■ ■ ■ ■

Profile

Dr. Caroll is an artificial intelligence created by the dataDyne Corp. with an emphasis on language skills and code breaking. Fortunately, he has morals, and due to his formidable level of intelligence, he has guessed some of dataDyne's plans. His voice is highly precise and educated and simulates the character of an academic.

dr. Caroll

Age: 6 months
Race: The Caroll Sapient (AI)

■ ■ ■ ■ ■ ■

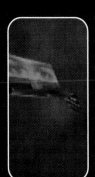

Profile

Head of the National Security Agency, he has a friendship with Cassandra De Vries, although it operates more like a partnership of interest. He tends to do what Cassandra says; although he has a dominant personality, it is not as dominant as hers. He serves as a figurehead for some of the rogue elements in the NSA.

trent easton

Age: 46 years 7 months
Race: Human (Male)

■ ■ ■ ■ ■ ■

Profile

A highly educated, shrewd African-American, he's trying to do what's right but is surrounded by people such as Trent Easton. He believes he has Trent under control after refusing the request for the loan of the *Pelagic II* to the dataDyne Corp. The majority of political commentators perceive him as being easily led, which is perhaps unfair.

the U.S. President

Age: 50 years
Race: Human (Male)

■ ■ ■ ■ ■ ■

PROFILE

An alien from the Maian race, he is a "Protector" (bodyguard) for the Maian ambassador who travels to Earth at Daniel Carrington's request. Protectors are trained to excel in the use of assorted weaponry. Elvis, a terraphile, finds Earth and everything about it fascinating.

ELVIS

AGE: 320 YEARS
RACE: MAIAN (MALE)

■■■■■■

PROFILE

MAIANS

The Maians are the race of aliens that have come to be known on Earth as "Greys." They have been monitoring Earth for several centuries and are benevolent toward mankind, sensing great potential in the human race. Their contact on Earth is Daniel Carrington. A formal political contact has yet to be made.

■■■■■■

PROFILE

This is a Skedar warrior lurking within a holographic projection of a striking young blonde human male in his late 20s. The oral modulation unit gives the Skedar a precise, persuasive, and intelligent voice. It is an unusually subtle propaganda tool for the Skedar.

MR. BLONDE

AGE: UNKNOWN
RACE: SKEDAR (DISGUISED)

■■■■■■

PROFILE

SKEDAR WARRIORS

The Skedar are a warlike alien race who have fought the Maians for centuries and have only recently agreed to a cease-fire. They are small snakelike creautures, so they tend to use mechanized armatures to walk about and fight in. They're very aggressive; they've made war a religion and are extremely devout.

■■■■■■

LOCATIONS

AIR FORCE ONE

The President's airplane. This particular *Air Force One* is optimized for cold climates, useful when it is based in the north of Alaska. The flight destination is Oslo, Norway.

PROFILES

Alaskan Air Base

Brooks Range, Alaska. This is one of a series of reinforced air bases available as staging posts for *Air Force One*. Typically, air bases are in remote, inhospitable regions, far away from prying eyes.

Area 51

Near Groom Dry Lake, Nevada. This is a section of the extensive facility known as Area 51. Exterior helipads and communication towers hint at the size of the complex beneath ground level.

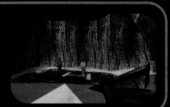

Carrington Institute

Base of operations. The Institute building is composed of many different areas: offices and laboratories, workshops and hangars. It is quite isolated from the outside world, which helps keep the operations covert.

Carrington Villa

Private coastal retreat. Owned by the Institute, this secluded residence is used by Daniel Carrington as a retreat from the pressures of the Institute. It has an observatory and a power generator, as well as an extensive wine cellar.

Cetan Ship

The most alien environment on Earth. This huge ship of alien construction has lain on the ocean floor for millions of years.

Chicago

Back streets of the city. A seedy, grimy part of the city of Chicago, now closed to ground traffic. It is here that the G5 Corporation has its headquarters.

PROFILES

CRASH SITE

Victoria Island 71°N, 118°W. In the rocky snow-covered landscape of the Arctic Circle, the wreckage of the stricken plane has come to rest.

G5 BUILDING

G5 Headquarters. Inside the G5 building is a meeting room protected by anti-recording safeguards. This is the most secure place for dataDyne to formulate confidential plans.

LABORATORY BASEMENT

Underground research labs. These heavily guarded, well-hidden labs hold the key to dataDyne's future. Within them, techs work on top-secret projects aimed at putting dataDyne on the top of the heap.

LUCERNE TOWER

Global headquarters. In the midst of the business district, the austere skyscraper of the dataDyne Corporation stands out from the surroundings.

PELAGIC II

Specialized deep-sea research ship. Owned by the U.S. government, the *Pelagic II* can stage deep-sea diving operations in all weather conditions. It's the world's only fully integrated ocean floor research vessel.

SKEDAR ASSAULT SHIP

Troop-carrying spacecraft. An interplanetary assault ship that carries Skedar warriors to their war zones, it's part of the much-reduced Skedar battle fleet.

SKEDAR HOMEWORLD

The planet of the Battle Shrine. It is part of a complex solar system that includes three suns.

VEHICLES

A51 Interceptor

Robotic air interceptor. A robotic variant of the HoverBike with more powerful AG and turbine units, it can reach Mach 2 with ease, yet can cruise for hours at a walking pace. Although quite well armed, it relies on maneuverability rather than shielding.

Cleaning HovBot

Your helpful buddy. This device keeps the place clean and tidy. Because it usually has access to all areas of a building, agents are advised to leave such robots intact whenever possible; they can unwittingly provide a means of ingress to sensitive zones.

G5 Robot

Urban combat droid. A combat robot designed for urban warfare, it uses an AG unit to hover and is heavily armed and shielded. It's often used to keep out unwanted visitors, due to its "shoot first and don't ask questions later" programming.

HoverBike

Low altitude vehicle. A patrol bike, it uses a small AG unit to hover, then a small but powerful turbine with vectored thrust to move and provide directional control.

Hovercopter

Urban AG gunship. An urban patrol and suppression vehicle with a two-man crew, it's armed with a Vulcan cannon on the nose pod, and two wingtip-mounted dumbfire missile pods. It can be taken out with sustained gunfire or, preferably, one well-aimed rocket.

HoverCrate

Gravity-negation device. Designed to aid warehouse workers, it is attached to the side of a crate. When activated, the AG field lifts the crate, cutting down on some of the inertia.

Jumpship

Agile troop craft. This small, fast, highly maneuverable agent-deployment craft was designed for use in urban areas. It can be either computer controlled or remote piloted and has enough room inside for three to four agents, plus equipment.

Maian Vessel

Scout and patrol vessel. Because it's designed to carry a single Maian pilot, a passenger would feel cramped—a human passenger even more so.

Skedar Shuttle

Alien troop dropship. Capable of carrying 10 fully armed and armored Skedar warriors to battle, it's undetectable by conventional radar. It can broadcast powerful jamming waves over a considerable area; these disrupt communications and detection equipment.

WEAPONS

AR34

Affiliation: Carrington
Primary: Burst Fire
Secondary: Use Scope
Magazine Capacity: 30
Average Fire Rate: 750 RPM

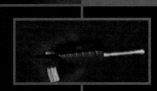

The Carrington Institute's main Assault Rifle. A good range and magazine size make it a useful weapon; the secondary mode enables the user to move while zoomed in on a target.

CALLISTO NTG

Affiliation: Maian
Primary: Rapid Fire
Secondary: High Impact Shells
Magazine Capacity: 32
Average/Secondary Fire Rate: 900/300 RPM

Another example of excellent Maian firearm design. It can fire standard shots as fast as any other submachine gun (SMG), or it can fire high velocity rounds which will easily penetrate objects to find targets hiding in cover. The only drawbacks with the secondary fire mode are that the fire rate is lower and the accuracy suffers from the power of the shot.

CMP150

Affiliation: dataDyne
Primary: Rapid Fire
Secondary: Follow Lock-On
Magazine Capacity: 32
Average Fire Rate: 900 RPM

A dataDyne classic and a bestseller, this submachine gun boasts a 32 round mag and a special feature—the ability to designate and lock on to targets in the line of sight. It turns an average marksman into an excellent one, provided he or she is clever enough to operate the gun.

COMBAT KNIFE

Affiliation: dataDyne
Primary: Knife Slash
Secondary: Throw Poison Knife
Throwing Capacity: 2

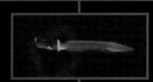

A large and vicious combat knife. It contains a vial of poison that shatters when thrown, giving a wounded enemy at most 6 seconds to live. A dataDyne weapon through and through.

CROSSBOW

Affiliation: Carrington
Primary: Sedate
Secondary: Instant Kill
Magazine Capacity: 10

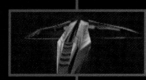

This Crossbow is a short-range pistol-sized example, mounted on a Carrington Institute agent's wrist. It folds up to aid concealment and can fire up to five bolts, either the more usual drugged shots, or a lethal bolt.

CYCLONE

Affiliation: Chesluk Industries
Primary: Rapid Fire
Secondary: Magazine Discharge
Magazine Capacity: 50
Average/Secondary Fire Rate: 900/2000 RPM

Designed for use by bodyguards, the Cyclone has been adopted by presidential security due to its excellent capability when used for suppression. In extreme circumstances, it can more than double its fire rate, discharging the magazine in a second.

DEVASTATOR

Affiliation: dataDyne
Primary: Grenade Launcher
Secondary: Wall Hugger
Magazine Capacity: 8

A long range Grenade delivery system manufactured by dataDyne. The secondary fire mode coats the Grenades with a sticky substance; when fired, the bomb attaches itself to wall or ceiling. After a few seconds, it detaches to fall to the ground, where it detonates.

DRAGON

Affiliation: dataDyne
Primary: Rapid Fire
Secondary: Proximity Self Destruct
Magazine Capacity: 30
Average Fire Rate: 700 RPM

A standard Assault Rifle with an evil twist—when the secondary mode is activated, it becomes a proximity-activated mine that looks like a gun.

DY357 MAGNUM

Affiliation: dataDyne
Primary: Single Shot
Secondary: Pistol Whip
Magazine Capacity: 6

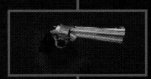

The dataDyne DY357 is the most powerful handgun in the world. Each round has an impressive penetration factor and knocks the target back with the weight and power of the shot. Custom models are made for valued clients; NSA Director Trent Easton is rumored to have a gold plated variant.

DY357-LX

Affiliation: dataDyne
Primary: Single Shot
Secondary: Pistol Whip
Magazine Capacity: 6

The DY357-LX was custom built for NSA Director Trent Easton. Besides boasting an attractive genuine tiger skin grip, this golden gun features a velocity optimized barrel, meaning that each bullet always meets its target with fatal force.

FALCON 2

Affiliation: Carrington
Primary: Single Shot
Secondary: Pistol Whip
Magazine Capacity: 8

Accurate and trustworthy, this gun is the workhorse of the Institute's operations. Use the laser sight to place bullets with deadly effect, or pistol-whip adversaries to knock them out.

FALCON 2 (SILENCER)

Affiliation: Carrington
Primary: Single Shot
Secondary: Pistol Whip
Magazine Capacity: 8

An upgraded Falcon 2 that has the added benefit of being silent, but deadly.

FALCON 2 (SCOPE)

Affiliation: Carrington
Primary: Single Shot
Secondary: Pistol Whip
Magazine Capacity: 8

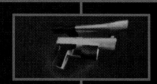

An upgraded Falcon 2, featuring a 2x magnification scope that allows you to take advantage of the Falcon's superior accuracy.

FARSIGHT XR-20

Affiliation: Maian
Primary: Rail-gun Effect
Secondary: Target Locator
Magazine Capacity: 8

The FarSight rifle is a Maian hybrid of an X-ray scanning device coupled with a rifle that can shoot through solid objects. The scope can lock onto and track life sources, though the device does not pan as fast as a running enemy can move.

GRENADE

Affiliation: Carrington
Primary: 4-Second Fuse
Secondary: Proximity Pinball
Maximum: 12

An updated version of the trusty grenade. Can be thrown with a four-second fuse or used as a bouncing proximity bomb.

K7 AVENGER

Affiliation: dataDyne
Primary: Burst Fire
Secondary: Threat Detector
Magazine Capacity: 25
Average Fire Rate: 950 RPM

Another piece of a high-tech kit from dataDyne. Ordinarily an assault rifle with a smallish magazine and a powerful punch, it has a threat detection mode that highlights explosives, wallguns, and similar hazards.

LAPTOP GUN

Affiliation: Carrington
Primary: Burst Fire
Secondary: Deploy as Sentry Gun
Magazine Capacity: 50
Average Fire Rate: 1000 RPM

A submachine gun made to look like a laptop PC. In disguised form, the gun cannot fire, but when activated, it unfolds into shape. The PC gun will not bear close inspection; it will boot up, but the memory is a quarter of what it is supposed to be.

LASER

Affiliation: Carrington
Primary: Pulse Fire
Secondary: Short Range Stream

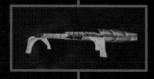

The Laser is wrist-mounted and deadly accurate. It can either fire long-range pulses, or it can sustain a constant, concentrated stream of energy at short range.

MAGSEC 4

Affiliation: Chesluk Industries
Primary: Single Shot
Secondary: 3-Round Burst
Magazine Capacity: 9

A state-of-the-art military pistol, largely used by peace-keeping forces. It has a slight zoom capability, and boasts a 3-round burst secondary fire mode.

MAULER

Affiliation: Skedar
Primary: Single Shot
Secondary: Charge-Up Shot
Magazine Capacity: 20

If you see a Skedar coming at you, the chances are it's carrying one of these. A large magazine and a bladed barrel make the pistol a formidable handgun, but the killer blow comes from the secondary function—charge the shot up for extra power at the cost of a few rounds of ammo.

PHOENIX

Affiliation: Maian
Primary: Single Shot
Secondary: Explosive Shells
Magazine Capacity: 8

The Maian standard issue sidearm. A flexible gun, the pistol fires standard shots, or explosive shots at no cost to the rest of the magazine.

PROXIMITY MINE

Affiliation: Carrington
Primary: Proximity Explosive
Secondary: Threat Detector
Maximum: 10

A mine with a proximity fuse. It has a threat detection/evaluation sensor that can be activated as a secondary mode.

RC-P120

Affiliation: Chesluk Industries
Primary: Rapid Fire
Secondary: Cloak
Magazine Capacity: 120
Average Fire Rate: 1100 RPM

The Carrington Institute's secret weapon. It fires at a phenomenal rate and has a huge magazine capacity. The secondary mode is a Cloaking Device that runs off the ammunition in the magazine. A devastating weapon.

REAPER

Affiliation: Skedar
Primary: Reapage
Secondary: Grinder
Magazine Capacity: 200
Maximum Fire Rate: 1800 RPM

A truly terrifying weapon in the hands of someone strong enough to control the massive recoil; for anyone else, a highly unwieldy but effective corridor clearance weapon.

REMOTE MINE

Affiliation: Carrington
Primary: Remote Explosive
Secondary: Detonate
Maximum: 10

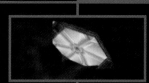

A mine that can be triggered remotely. The Remote Mine can be detonated by pressing Ⓐ and Ⓑ simultaneously. This is quicker and allows you to explode mines in the air after you throw them.

ROCKET LAUNCHER

Affiliation: dataDyne
Primary: Rocket Launcher
Secondary: Targeted Rocket
Magazine Capacity: 1

A cumbersome weapon. Fires either a standard rocket or a slower, homing rocket when locked on to the unfortunate target.

SHOTGUN

Affiliation: dataDyne
Primary: Shotgun Fire
Secondary: Double Blast
Magazine Capacity: 9

A dataDyne weapon manufactured for security forces. A nine-cartridge magazine combined with single or double fire modes make it a dangerous close-quarters weapon.

SLAYER

Affiliation: Skedar
Primary: Rocket Launcher
Secondary: Fly-by-Wire Rocket
Magazine Capacity: 1

The Skedar enjoy seeing the terror of their enemies. It seems natural that they should have a remote-controlled rocket as a secondary fire mode on their basic Rocket Launcher, so that they can take pleasure from the prey's vain attempts to escape the closing projectile. Holding down the Ⓡ in Fly-by-Wire mode will slow the rocket in flight for better maneuverability.

SNIPER RIFLE

Affiliation: Carrington
Primary: Single Shot
Secondary: Crouch
Magazine Capacity: 8

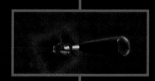

With a powerful zoom and a high velocity bullet, this Carrington Institute weapon is one of the best Sniper Rifles ever made. Crouch down for perfect accuracy.

SUPERDRAGON

Affiliation: dataDyne
Primary: Rapid Fire
Secondary: Grenade Launcher
Magazine Capacity: 30/6
Average Fire Rate: 700 RPM

A variant of the Dragon Assault Rifle—instead of a proximity explosive, it has a small grenade launcher. Excellent support weapon.

TIMED MINE

Affiliation: Carrington
Primary: Timed Explosive
Secondary: Threat Detector
Maximum: 10

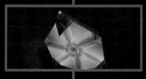

A mine with a short timed fuse. It has a threat detection/evaluation sensor that can be activated as a secondary mode.

TRANQUILIZER

Affiliation: Carrington
Primary: Sedate
Secondary: Lethal Injection
Magazine Capacity: 8

A rapid-fire device, it can be used as a weapon in an emergency, but it is designed primarily as a dermal spray injector for sedative drugs. Users are advised that a full discharge of the drug reservoir can be fatal.

devices

CAMSPY

A tiny remote camera for stealthy exploration. Equipped for spectroscopic holography. Opens doors by projecting a human-sized pulse of heat. Also available in BombSpy and DrugSpy models. Operate by pressing Ⓩ to take a holograph. Pressing Ⓑ will open any doors in the way. Hold down Ⓡ to look around.

Item Tip

The CamSpy is not invisible—enemies may spot it—so be careful when entering an inhabited area. Remember that the CamSpy will remain where you left it unless you pick it up.

CLOAKING DEVICE

Disrupts the visible spectrum of light around the wearer, creating an almost perfect chameleonlike effect. This field is disrupted when the wearer fires. Selecting the Cloaking Device from your inventory will activate it. Reselect to deactivate.

Item Tip

Don't waste the Cloaking Device when there is no one around to observe you. Avoid firing unless absolutely necessary and until you are assured of the success of your attack.

COMBAT BOOST

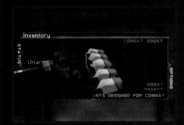

Stimulants designed for combat applications. When administered, Combat Boosts seem to slow down the passage of time to give a reaction window.

Item Tip

Reloading and switching weapons takes forever. Use the Quick menu to switch weapons to avoid switching to the wrong one. Be sure to call up the Quick menu immediately after using the Boost.

DATA UPLINK

Provides a link from the field agent to the Institute hackers back at HQ, who can then download data or crack electronic locks remotely. Stand next to a terminal and press Ⓑ when holding the Data Uplink.

item tip

ALWAYS KEEP THE TARGET OBJECT IN VIEW WHEN USING THE DATA UPLINK, AND STAY CLOSE TO PREVENT THE CONNECTION FROM BEING SEVERED.

DISGUISE

Allay suspicion by the use of a Disguise. But always be alert for the possibility of being unmasked by a quick-witted enemy. To wear the Disguise, simply select it from your inventory.

item tip

A DISGUISE IS NOT JUST THE CLOTHING, IT IS THE MANNER OF THE PERSON WEARING IT. DON'T BEHAVE OUT OF CHARACTER FOR THE PERSON YOU ARE TRYING TO BE.

DOOR DECODER

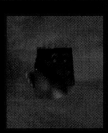

Stand-alone code-breaking device. Attaches to the control panel and sifts through the possible combinations until the lock is opened. Stand next to a door pad and press Ⓑ while holding the Door Decoder to use it.

item tip

IF YOU HAVE TROUBLE ATTACHING THE DECODER, TRY STANDING CLOSER TO THE TARGET AND FACING IT.

ECM MINE

Emits a constantly shifting signal designed to jam any electronic communications device. Must be placed on the object to be effective. Press Ⓩ to throw the mine. Hold down Ⓡ and move the Control Stick to fine-tune your aim before throwing.

item tip

BE SURE THE MINE WILL LAND IN THE CORRECT PLACE BY GETTING AS CLOSE AS YOU CAN TO THE TARGET. ADJUST YOUR AIM USING ©▲, ©▼, ©◀, AND ©► OR THE Ⓡ AIMING MODE.

IR SCANNER

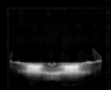

Translates thermal data into visible images. Can be used in darkness and will also reveal anomalies such as hidden doors and weak wall sections. Select the IR Scanner from your inventory to activate it. Reselect to deactivate.

Item Tip

The visor narrows your peripheral vision, which can cause problems in combat. Be sure of your situation before you use it.

NIGHT VISION

Enhances any visible light to produce an image of the surrounding area. Also highlights life forms. Overloads in normal light conditions, "whiting out" the display. Select the Night Vision from your inventory to activate it. Reselect to deactivate.

Item Tip

Useful in combat, but can cause problems when overloading. Try to anticipate such situations and react before the enemy does.

R-TRACKER

Locates a particular object on a HUD radar map. Shows the relative bearing and distance. Selecting the Tracker from your inventory will activate it. Reselect to deactivate.

Item Tip

The R-Tracker only indicates direction and relative height; it doesn't display a map guiding you to the target. Pay attention to your surroundings, and be prepared to explore.

X-RAY SCANNER

Used to look through solid walls and objects. Can see things that the Night Vision and IR Scanner cannot. Select the X-Ray Scanner from your inventory to activate it. Reselect to deactivate.

Item Tip

The X-Ray Scanner can't see things that are right up in your face. If you find that you can't see something that should be there, try backing up a few steps.

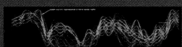

SIMULANTS

When it comes time to tackle the multiplayer games, it might be hard to get enough friends together to play. Never fear. The Simulants will fill the gaps when you have to play *now*!

There are different types of Simulant, and certain Sims are not immediately available. They must be opened up by playing the Challenges. This section will help you understand what you're up against.

Simulant Basics// There are a few general things you need to know before we jump into the specifics of each Simulant Type.

Where to Find Them// To set up specific Simulant teams for your multiplayer games, go to the Combat Simulator menu, then choose "Advanced Setup."

Choose "Simulants" and then "Add Simulant." Presto—you're there.

Changing Difficulty or Type// You can adjust the Difficulty or Type of Simulants once you've added them to your list. Highlight the Simulant you want to adjust and press Ⓐ. Highlight "Difficulty" and press Ⓐ again. Choose the rating you want from there.

Choosing Simulants// Now you've got choices to make. Do you want Normal Simulants or Special Simulants? In a nutshell, the Normal Simulants are all-around players named after their different Difficulty levels—EasySim, NormalSim, etc. The Special Simulants each have a unique "personality type" that guides their style of play.

How much of a challenge do you want?

Normal or Special? Choose from this menu.

NOTE Changing a Normal Simulant's Difficulty will simply change it into another Normal Simulant because they *are* their Difficulty. (There's no such thing as an EasySim set at Hard Difficulty.) However, a Special Simulant can be any Difficulty you want.

You can also change a Simulant's Type if the mood strikes you. Highlight "Change Type..." and press Ⓐ. Pick which Type you want to go up against from the

Each type and their foibles are described later in

Choosing Character// You can also make changes to a Simulant's appearance. In the same menu you use to change Difficulty and Type you'll find the "Character…" selection. Highlight it and press Ⓐ to see your choices.

Who do you want to be today?

A window pops up with a slowly rotating face. Moving the Control Stick left or right will move you through the different faces you can choose.

Move the Control Stick down and you'll see the body type of your Simulant. Some heads and bodies are only opened after certain Challenges. Again, moving left and right scrolls through the available bodies and costumes. Putting Mr. Blonde's head on Joanna's body is both possible and funny.

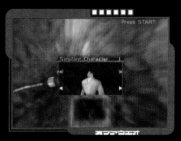

The possibilities are endless.

NOTE

In the Simulant descriptions below, we list the default character type for each. Familiarize yourself with them so that you know whether it's a ShieldSim or a KazeSim coming at you.

Simulant Types// Now it's time to familiarize yourself with the specifics of each Type of Simulant you can use. Here's all the game information you'll need to make an informed decision on whom you want running around with guns in your multiplayer games.

NOTE

Each Simulant Type has a unique default character body. For example, all PeaceSims start with the dataDyne Lab Technician body. When you have several Simulants of one type—such as three PeaceSims—the faces will be different on each one. Of course, you can change all that as described above.

NORMAL SIMULANTS

DarkSim
CHARACTER: DINNER JACKET

Prototype cyborg developed by dataDyne to counteract Carrington operatives. Remember that this Simulant, unlike all the others, is not human. This means that it may be able to do things a human cannot.

DarkSims are fast as lightning and have pinpoint accuracy. They also know the levels better than you do—maybe. Study up on the maps so you can arm yourself quickly and escape hopeless fights. Never stop moving and always keep looking at the radar. If you can beat a few DarkSims, then most of your friends will seem like fat, slow targets when you play them.

NOTE: When you've unlocked Challenge 28, DarkSim becomes available for your training pleasure

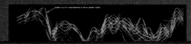

SIMULANTS

EasySim
CHARACTER: DATADYNE SECURITY

This Simulant has basic skills and intelligence, but it can still be dangerous.

Although a bit more aggressive than a MeatSim, the EasySim still won't test your abilities to the fullest. Feel free to stand still as you take aim.

HardSim
CHARACTER: DATADYNE SHOCK TROOPER

This Simulant is as skilled as a good human player.

HardSims will make you work, if not sweat. Against a single HardSim you'll need to choose your battlefield. They're quick and reasonably accurate. They won't rush headlong at you, but they won't turn their backs on you either. More than one of them will cause some headaches.

NOTE: **Once Challenge 11 is open you can use the HardSim in multiplayer games with three or more players.**

MeatSim
CHARACTER: DATADYNE INFANTRY

This is the easiest of all the Simulants to defeat and is, therefore, the best choice for the beginner. It is not very intelligent, and its shooting skills are very poor.

Not too bright or aggressive, slow, and a lousy shot. MeatSims are just that—meat. Take your time and pick your shots against these Simulants.

NormalSim
CHARACTER: DATADYNE TROOPER

This Simulant is as skilled as the average human player.

A NormalSim by itself won't give you much trouble. In a crowd and in tight spaces, however, you'll have a mild challenge.

PerfectSim
CHARACTER: NSA BODYGUARD

The ultimate adversary. The most intelligent and skilled Simulant. Most players will eventually want to use PerfectSim all the time as their skills improve.

As you'll see, there is a tougher Normal Simulant, but PerfectSims are deadly opponents and not to be taken lightly. They know every map. They know where you are, where all the weapons and shields are, and they'll move fast. Fighting them will sharpen your skills and frustrate you at times.

NOTE: **Unlocking Challenge 16 will allow you to select PerfectSim for your multiplayer games.**

PerfectSims and DarkSims are at their most frustrating in the Challenges. Their speed and ability to shoot up at a catwalk while running backward (among other almost inhuman skills) will test your patience. Keep training and you'll be able to best them. For a real workout, set up multiplayer scenarios against them in groups of three or more.

SPECIAL SIMULANTS

Coward Sim
CHARACTER: THE PRESIDENT

This Simulant does not really want to fight and will try to survive by running away. It may sometimes attack, but only if the opponent has an inferior weapon. Draw out a better gun or shoot it and it will run away!

CowardSim doesn't so much run away as it does "strategically retreat." That is, it will run backward to keep its distance from you while still firing at you. It's not a pacifist, it just doesn't want to die. So, keep an eye on your radar to avoid sneak attacks from these Simulants and try to run them down. Don't go after them unarmed, though, because they tend to grab for big weapons.

FeudSim
CHARACTER: NSA LACKEY

Once this Simulant picks a target, that player had better watch out! A FeudSim will pursue the player until the game is over! Even if it is killed, it will bear its grudge.

This Simulant is a fun one to throw into the mix. It will pick a target, as described above, and hunt it down constantly. This does not mean, however, that FeudSim will ignore a target of opportunity. It will still fire on other players, it just prefers to go after its chosen enemy. Don't bother it if it isn't after you and it'll hassle another player, leaving you to concentrate on others.

FistSim
CHARACTER: PELAGIC II GUARD

This Simulant protests the use of weapons in a similar way to the PeaceSims. However, it has no such reservations when it comes to unarmed combat. It will always try to use its fists to attack or disarm its opponent.

A FistSim can be annoying. When you confront one, keep away from it. Once it gets close it will go for a disarm and then circle and punch until you go down. If it gets close you'll spend a good deal of time with blurry vision. The best weapons against these guys are automatic rifles. The steady fire will brush them back. Act like a CowardSim; run backward and fire at the FistSim as it comes at you.

JudgeSim
CHARACTER: STEWARD

This Simulant has a strong sense of justice and despises the tactics of the PreySim. It will always try to kill the winning player in order to even up the score.

Even if you're not in the lead, JudgeSim is a concern. It has no compunction against taking the lead for itself. Keep a sharp eye out if you're on top. JudgeSim will then focus on you and you alone. If *it's* in the lead, though, it won't be picky about who it shoots. You can relax just a bit when someone else is leading.

KazeSim
CHARACTER: PRESIDENTIAL SECURITY

This Simulant will stop at nothing to destroy its target. It is very aggressive and never keeps its distance—even if it's holding a Grenade! Be very careful of an adversary who is not afraid to die.

KazeSims tend to run in straight lines. Their major objective is to get to you as quickly as possibly—with or without a weapon. On lower Difficulty levels, KazeSims will stand still while firing, allowing a quick player to take easy shots. Don't sell them short, however; KazeSims are relentless and can cut a wide swath through a multiplayer game.

PeaceSim
CHARACTER: DATADYNE LAB TECHNICIAN

These Simulants are scientists who protest the use of weapons. They will go around the level hunting for guns that are lying around and hoard them so that players cannot use them. Of course, if you were to shoot them, they might just drop a few!

PeaceSims are actually fun to have in a level. They're pests because they snap up weapons and ammo, but when you kill one, it will usually drop a mother lode of arms. A PeaceSim will run from you, so chase it down. If it gets in close, though, it will disarm you and then take off. PeaceSims aren't looking to make any kills. You could say they're moving weapon lockers.

PreySim
Character: dataDyne Shock Trooper

This Simulant prefers to prey on the weak in order to get easier kills. It will look for players who have just respawned, have an inferior weapon, or are low on health.

PreySims live up to their description. The PreySim will single out and attack the weakest of a group of players. This is good for you if you're not the weakest. The PreySim ignores the stronger players in the area, opening itself up to attack.

RocketSim
Character: G5 Guard

This Simulant loves to see things blow up. It prefers weapons that make big explosions over conventional handguns or automatics. This also extends to weapons that have explosive secondary functions!

RocketSim is rather one dimensional: it likes things that go boom. This doesn't mean that it won't use other weaponry, it just prefers the loud stuff. Use it with the Explosive, Grenade Launcher, or Rocket Launcher Weapons Sets to let it reach its full potential. The best way to use conventional weapons against its rocket or Grenade attacks is blanket-firing your own explosives. Keep an eye on your radar. When the RocketSim is about to turn a corner nearby, launch a bunch of Grenades into the door. More than likely it'll run right into the explosion.

ShieldSim
Character: G5 SWAT Guard

Always goes for maximum Shield protection. If this Simulant loses any Shield energy, it will go and search for a new Shield. Not much use if there are no Shields on the level!

Even if there aren't any Shields on a level, the ShieldSim will spawn with full Shield protection—it just can't be replenished. Don't think that if you shoot a ShieldSim once, it will simply turn its back on you and look for more Shields. It will run backward, firing at you as it goes. Keep this in mind as you chase down ShieldSims.

SpeedSim
Character: Mr. Blonde

These Simulants have been trained for speed. They can easily outrun a human player, so it's no use running away from a SpeedSim unless you know some good shortcuts!

Speedy they are, sturdy they are not. The SpeedSim is fast, but it tends to rely on Shields rather than evasive motion for its protection. Without a Shield, the SpeedSim will fall to a few solid shots. Accuracy will make your job easier against SpeedSims. Also, they tend to stop and fire if you're standing still. Toe-to-toe is not the best situation, but if you need a moment to lock on, stop and SpeedSim will stop with you.

SIMULANTS

TurtleSim
CHARACTER: DANIEL CARRINGTON

This Simulant wears a prototype Shield generator developed by dataDyne scientists. The generator projects a protective Shield around its host that has twice the strength of a normal Shield. Unfortunately, this restricts the host's movement, so it can only move at a slow pace. TurtleSims carry this Shield as standard even if there are no Shields on the level.

A tough, tough Shield surrounds this Simulant. Punching through it requires a lot of ammo. Even Devastator Grenades don't do the trick in one shot. The best remedy is sustained machine gun fire and a Shield of your own. Double CMP150s do the trick handily. Remember that slow doesn't mean stupid. A TurtleSim is going to fire back. Don't expect an easy kill.

VengeSim
CHARACTER: ALASKAN GUARD

Be careful if you shoot or kill a VengeSim because it always attacks the player who last killed it.

This is a very straightforward Simulant. Kill it and it will come after you. It's like a FeudSim-lite. It won't carry a grudge for the whole game—just until it manages to avenge one death.

PERFECT DARK™

the carrington institute

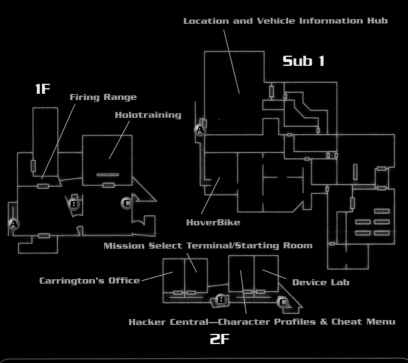

1F
- Firing Range
- Holotraining
- HoverBike
- Mission Select Terminal/Starting Room
- Carrington's Office
- Device Lab
- Hacker Central—Character Profiles & Cheat Menu

Sub 1
- Location and Vehicle Information Hub

2F

The circled letters (Ⓐ) show where the different floors connect. They indicate stairs, ramps, elevators, even holes in the ground.

HACKER CENTRAL ★ ★ ★

This room houses two computers. The computer on the left houses dossiers on some of the major players in the game. You can also find this information in the Character Profiles section of this book.

The second computer allows you to access the various cheats you have unlocked throughout the game. These can also be accessed via the in-game menu.

DEVICE LAB ★ ★ ★

The Carrington Institute technicians in this room provide training on the various devices you'll encounter in the game.

DATA UPLINK

Use the Data Uplink to hack the terminal in the corner, unlocking a secret door. Pick up the Data Link from the table, and walk to the computer terminal on the left side of the room. Look at the terminal and activate the Data Uplink.

ECM MINE

Throw the ECM Mine onto the lighting hub located through the secret door. Pick up the ECM Mine from the table. Walk through the secret door and take the first right. Head to the opening at the end of the hall. Throw the ECM Mine through the opening so it attaches to the lighting hub.

CamSpy

Holograph the hacker's terminal next door in the Information Lab. Pick up the CamSpy from the table and equip it. Maneuver the CamSpy to the red grate next to the computer table. Open the grate and proceed through. Make your way through the air duct to the Information Lab. (Stay in the air duct until you hit the next red grate.) Take a snapshot of the computer on the left.

Night Vision

Head into the darkness, find the light switch, and activate it to turn the lights back on. Pick up the Night Vision glasses from the table. Do *not* equip them in a lighted room. Head through the door and into the hallway. Veer left. When the area gets too dark to see, equip the Night Vision. Enter the next room and look to your right to find the light switch.

THE CARRINGTON INSTITUTE

DOOR DECODER

Find the pad by the locked door and use the Door Decoder on it to unlock the door. Pick up the Door Decoder and head through the secret door. Take the first right, then the next left. Attach the Door Decoder to the lock.

R-TRACKER

Activate the R-Tracker and follow the radar signature to retrieve the item. Pick up the R-Tracker from the table and head through the secret door. Follow the radar to the object: take a right, then a left. The IR Scanner is down the second left-hand corridor.

IR SCANNER

Turning on the IR Scanner, find the hidden door and open it. Pick up the IR Scanner and head through the secret door. Take a right, then a left. Activate the IR Scanner after you pass through the red grate. Take the first left, then go all the way down the hall and take another left. The secret door you're looking for is bright red.

X-RAY SCANNER

With the X-Ray Scanner on, search for the two hidden switches and activate them to turn off the laser grid. Pick up the X-Ray Scanner and head through the secret door. Proceed to the second secret door. Follow the corridor to the first open room. Equip the X-Ray Scanner and look to your left and right. There you will find both switches.

DISGUISE

Grimshaw has a Cloaking Device waiting to be serviced. Head next door and use the Disguise to "acquire" it from him! Pick up the Disguise and equip it. Go through the red grate next to the computer terminal. Follow the duct to the Information Lab. Talk to Grimshaw.

CLOAKING DEVICE

Activate the Cloaking Device and head to Carrington's office to surprise him! Pick up the Cloaking Device and head through the secret door. Proceed to the second secret door. Follow the corridor until you reach the hall with the camera. Equip the Cloaking Device. Proceed down the corridor to Daniel Carrington's room. Tap him on the shoulder or wait until the Cloaking Device wears off.

FIRING RANGE GENERAL TIPS

— Hitting the bull's-eye does not break targets faster.

— The number of hits it takes to destroy targets is dependent on the weapon being used and the test being attempted.

— Reload while targets are flipped.

— Crouching steadies your aim and improves accuracy. Using ◎◀ and ◎▶ to strafe while facing a target is very useful.

— It doesn't matter how many times you attempt a test; for targets that have patterned movements, concentrate on watching the pattern on your first attempt so you know for later attempts how the targets move.

— You can shoot your weapon before the clock starts—line up your shot and get some licks in before the target moves.

— To help maintain accuracy, shoot at targets as they are moving straight toward you or going straight away from you (whenever possible).

— Practice, practice, practice: the more accurate you are with a weapon, the easier these tests are going to be. Practice making smooth movements with the Control Stick.

— When targets overlap, have patience; lay off the trigger until the bull's-eyes are lined up.

— Completeing the Firing Range—all 32 weapons—on any difficulty opens the Duel (a solo mission).

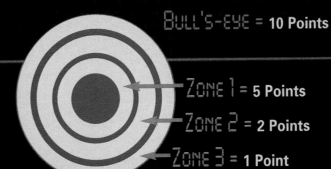

Bull's-Eye = 10 Points

Zone 1 = 5 Points

Zone 2 = 2 Points

Zone 3 = 1 Point

NOTE

You can complete most of the bronze tests with relative ease. They are used mainly to get a feel for the rate of fire, control, and general feel of the weapon.

target characteristics

Stationary: Targets stay in opening location and don't move

Stationary Pattern: Targets don't move, but they pop up in a set pattern

Left/Right: Targets move together horizontally

Left/Right Pattern: Targets move horizontally, but one or more move in an independent pattern

Back/Forth: Targets move away and back to you in a straight line (all together)

Back/Forth Pattern: Targets move toward and away from you, but one or more move in an independent pattern

Pattern: Targets move in a set pattern around the firing range

Flip: Targets flip around, making them unbreakable

FALCON 2

The Falcon 2 is a very accurate handgun, so any error in this test is your own. The secondary mode is a pistol-whip and is, therefore, useless in a firing range.

Goal Score:	120
Time Limit:	2m 0s

Goal Score:	80
Time Limit:	15s

Goal Score:	170
Time Limit:	10s
Ammo Limit:	24

FALCON 2 (SILENCER)

The silenced version of the Falcon 2 is an excellent stealth weapon designed to give you the advantage of surprise over your opponents. Test your accuracy to ensure that you never waste your chances.

⭐	**GOAL SCORE:** 120 **TIME LIMIT:** 2m 0s

TARGET CHARACTERISTICS: Flip

⭐	**GOAL SCORE:** 30 **GOAL TARGETS:** 9 **TIME LIMIT:** 2m 0s

TARGET CHARACTERISTICS: Flip

NOTES: Line up with each row of targets, then blast 'em in the center.

⭐	**GOAL SCORE:** 80 **GOAL TARGETS:** 3 **TIME LIMIT:** 30s

TARGET CHARACTERISTICS: Left/Right; Flip

NOTES: Reload while targets are flipped.

FALCON 2 (SCOPE)

To make better use of the accuracy of the Falcon 2, a scope has been attached to the pistol. As with the unmodified Falcon 2, the pistol-whip secondary mode is useless during the firing range test.

⭐	**GOAL SCORE:** 120 **TIME LIMIT:** 2m 0s

TARGET CHARACTERISTICS: Pattern

⭐	**GOAL SCORE:** 120 **MIN. ACCURACY:** 80% **TIME LIMIT:** 2m 0s

TARGET CHARACTERISTICS: Pattern

NOTES: To help maintain accuracy, shoot at targets as they are coming straight at you or going straight away from you.

⭐	**GOAL SCORE:** 80 **TIME LIMIT:** 10s **AMMO LIMIT:** 8

TARGET CHARACTERISTICS: Left/Right

NOTES: Must hit eight bull's-eyes. Strafe to line yourself up with the target when it stops at left and right. Shoot only when the target has stopped moving.

MAGSEC 4

The MagSec 4 has excellent shot power at the cost of accuracy, especially when used in the 3-round burst secondary mode. The only serious drawback to the weapon is a limited magazine size.

⭐	**GOAL SCORE:** 135 **TIME LIMIT:** 2m 0s

⭐	**GOAL SCORE:** 135 **TIME LIMIT:** 2m 0s **AMMO LIMIT:** 18

⭐	**GOAL SCORE:** 80 **GOAL TARGETS:** 4 **TIME LIMIT:** 12s

MAULER

This is a typical Skedar weapon, brutal and powerful. By sacrificing some of the magazine, the shot can be charged up to give a devastating blast. The large ammo capacity is a bonus.

GOAL SCORE:	200
TIME LIMIT:	2m 0s

TARGET CHARACTERISTICS: Back/Forth; Pattern

GOAL TARGETS:	8
TIME LIMIT:	2m 0s
AMMO LIMIT:	50

TARGET CHARACTERISTICS: Pattern

NOTES: Take your time and don't waste ammo. Also use the secondary charge-up mode.

GOAL TARGETS:	6
TIME LIMIT:	15s
AMMO LIMIT:	35

TARGET CHARACTERISTICS: Flip; Pattern

NOTES: Charge up the secondary mode while the targets are flipped.

PHOENIX

This versatile pistol gives two different delivery systems for the rounds it fires: a standard shot or an explosive round. Maian engineers managed to do this without compromising the energy usage of the weapon, though the fire rate is reduced.

GOAL SCORE:	90
TIME LIMIT:	2m 0s

TARGET CHARACTERISTICS: Flip; Pattern

GOAL TARGETS:	8
TIME LIMIT:	2m 0s
AMMO LIMIT:	18

TARGET CHARACTERISTICS: Flip; Left/Right; Pattern

NOTES: Use the secondary mode for one-shot, one-kill mayhem.

GOAL TARGETS:	6
TIME LIMIT:	20s
AMMO LIMIT:	3

TARGET CHARACTERISTICS: Pattern

NOTES: Use the secondary mode. Targets move every two seconds. Aim to hit each set of two as the targets converge.

DY357 MAGNUM

The key to the DY357 is in knowing when to reload. A six-round magazine means that you must always be alert in a firefight. The weight of the handgun can be useful if you have to club someone with it.

GOAL SCORE:	90
TIME LIMIT:	2m 0s

TARGET CHARACTERISTICS: Flip; Pattern

GOAL SCORE:	80
TIME LIMIT:	2m 0s
AMMO LIMIT:	3

TARGET CHARACTERISTICS: Stationary

NOTES: Three shots; nine targets. You must line up each shot to hit the bull's-eye of all three targets in a row.

GOAL SCORE:	50
TIME LIMIT:	12s
AMMO LIMIT:	5

TARGET CHARACTERISTICS: Flip

NOTES: Need five bull's-eyes with five shots.

DY357-LX

Trent Easton is always looking for that extra edge, and this gun's no exception. The bullets are as special as the rest of the gun; they are designed to shatter inside opponents to take them down quickly.

⭐	**Goal Score:** 90
	Time Limit: 2m 0s

Target Characteristics: Pattern

⭐	**Goal Score:** 200
	Time Limit: 30s

Target Characteristics: Left/Right Pattern

Notes: Move to the right and line up with the two targets at the beginning. Shoot through the bull's-eye of the two targets lined up. Use remaining shells on single target so the gun reloads as set of two targets are lining up.

⭐	**Goal Score:** 100
	Time Limit: 50s
	Ammo Limit: 12

Target Characteristics: Flip; Left/Right

Notes: Must hit bull's-eyes as target is moving. Smooth Control Stick movement is the key.

CMP150

A reliable and effective submachine gun, it is not difficult to see why this is the best-selling dataDyne weapon of the past two years even if the secondary mode is not taken into account. The target designate and lock-on system is excellent, and you should familiarize yourself with the complete operation of the weapon.

⭐	**Goal Score:** 240
	Time Limit: 2m 0s

Target Characteristics: Flip

⭐	**Goal Targets:** 4
	Time Limit: 2m 0s
	Ammo Limit: 80

Target Characteristics: Flip; Pattern

Notes: Don't waste ammo or worry about hitting in the center. Reload while the targets are flipped and break 'em when they're not.

⭐	**Goal Score:** 350
	Goal Targets: 6
	Time Limit: 20s

Target Characteristics: Pattern

Notes: Line up with the left target and shoot the targets as they come toward you. Be fast and accurate.

CYCLONE

The Cyclone submachine gun was specifically designed *not* to be accurate, though it is worth your time practicing. It can put a lot of bullets out in a short time, however, and is an excellent suppression weapon because of it.

⭐	**Goal Score:** 750
	Time Limit: 2m 0s

Target Characteristics: Stationary

⭐	**Goal Targets:** 5
	Time Limit: 20s

Target Characteristics: Back/Forth

Notes: Line up with each row of targets and mow them down.

⭐	**Goal Score:** 400
	Goal Target: 1
	Time Limit: 18s

Target Characteristics: Left/Right

Notes: Accuracy is important to rack up the necessary points.

CALLISTO NTG

Maian flexibility in design has produced this submachine gun with an interesting secondary mode—a high-velocity bullet that can penetrate objects easily. The fire rate, as with the Phoenix, is reduced during the secondary mode; this is to prevent damage to the firing mechanism and barrel.

GOAL SCORE:	480
TIME LIMIT:	2m 0s

TARGET CHARACTERISTICS: Stationary

GOAL SCORE:	1
TIME LIMIT:	30s

TARGET CHARACTERISTICS: Three front targets act as shields; back target moves Left/Right.

NOTES: Use the secondary mode to shoot through the shielding targets.

GOAL SCORE:	250
GOAL TARGETS:	2
TIME LIMIT:	20s

TARGET CHARACTERISTICS: Flip

NOTES: Reload while targets are flipped. Accuracy is important to get enough points to pass.

RC-P120

The RC-P120 fires a special mineral bullet that, coupled with a high fire rate and a huge magazine, makes this a perfect tool to be used against the Skedar, should the need arise. The bullets can be used to fuel a prototype Cloaking Device—the training has been altered to reflect this particular characteristic.

GOAL SCORE:	1000
TIME LIMIT:	2m 0s

TARGET CHARACTERISTICS: Stationary

GOAL SCORE:	300
TIME LIMIT:	20s

TARGET CHARACTERISTICS: Flip; Cloak Activated

NOTES: Activating the Cloaking Device will trigger targets to flip.

GOAL TARGETS:	9
TIME LIMIT:	20s
AMMO LIMIT:	180

TARGET CHARACTERISTICS: Flip; Cloak Activated

NOTES: Activate the Cloaking Device to take out front targets, then blast the remaining targets. Try strafing—accuracy is not a factor, but don't waste ammo.

LAPTOP GUN

Not only can the gun fold up to resemble a laptop PC, but it can be deployed as a sentry gun in secondary mode to cover an escape route or protect a location.

GOAL SCORE:	750
TIME LIMIT:	30s

TARGET CHARACTERISTICS: Stationary

GOAL SCORE:	90
GOAL TARGETS:	3
TIME LIMIT:	20s

TARGET CHARACTERISTICS: Flipped

NOTES: Use the secondary mode—deploy as a Sentry Gun. Throw the gun toward the left or right of the targets and it will automatically destroy the necessary targets.

GOAL SCORE:	750
GOAL TARGETS:	2
TIME LIMIT:	15s
AMMO LIMIT:	250

TARGET CHARACTERISTICS: Pattern

NOTES: Line up with the right target and hit the centers of the targets as they move away from you. Focus on destroying the first two while using the third to pick up points. After the first target breaks, strafe to the left to finish the second one off.

DRAGON

This is the model that dataDyne successfully submitted to the U.S. military, though it has yet to be widely adopted. In keeping with the tendency of dataDyne to give people nasty surprises, the basic model Assault Rifle carries a Proximity Mine below the barrel. Using the secondary mode rather obviously means you have to throw the weapon away.

GOAL SCORE:	450
TIME LIMIT:	2m 0s

TARGET CHARACTERISTICS: Flip

GOAL TARGETS:	1
TIME LIMIT:	10s
AMMO LIMIT:	1

TARGET CHARACTERISTICS: Back/Forth

NOTES: Use the Proximity Mine mode and throw the gun next to the target.

GOAL SCORE:	500
MIN. ACCURACY:	90%
TIME LIMIT:	15s

TARGET CHARACTERISTICS: Flip; Left/Right Pattern

NOTES: Use Aiming mode and track the slow target. This will allow you to hit the slow target as well as the front one.

K7 AVENGER

As far as we can ascertain, the secondary mode of the weapon seems to be a threat identifier, targeting mines, hidden explosive devices (such as the Dragon in secondary mode), and automatic guns. Though a powerful gun, the Assault Rifle's magazine is perhaps too small.

GOAL SCORE:	375
TIME LIMIT:	2m 0s

TARGET CHARACTERISTICS: Stationary Pattern

GOAL TARGETS:	4
TIME LIMIT:	2m 0s
AMMO LIMIT:	4

TARGET CHARACTERISTICS: Stationary Pattern

NOTES: Use the Threat Identifier to pick out the explosive targets.

GOAL TARGETS:	3
TIME LIMIT:	15s
AMMO LIMIT:	30

TARGET CHARACTERISTICS: Flip

NOTES: Each bullet must hit a target (10 rounds per target to break it; use any more and you will fail). Middle target flips first; hit it until it flips, then focus on left and right targets. Any wasted ammo causes failure; reload while targets are flipped.

AR34

The Institute's first attempt at a support weapon, the AR34 is a fairly basic Assault Rifle. The secondary mode is a permanent zoom. Testing is weighted toward accuracy training.

⭐	GOAL SCORE:	450
	TIME LIMIT:	2m 0s

TARGET CHARACTERISTICS: Back/Forth

⭐	GOAL TARGETS:	9
	TIME LIMIT:	2m 0s
	AMMO LIMIT:	120

TARGET CHARACTERISTICS: Pattern

NOTES: Take your time and don't waste ammo.

⭐	GOAL SCORE:	500
	MIN. ACCURACY:	100%
	TIME LIMIT:	20s

TARGET CHARACTERISTICS: Right/Left

NOTES: Double crouch down two blocks right of the kiosk. Activate the Use Scope. Then use the cursor to determine the position of the bull's-eye. The target will stay for about three seconds before it moves. Unload as many bullets as you can when it stops. Reload as it goes to the other side. Then repeat the process.

SUPERDRAGON

The heavier variant of the Dragon, with the proximity mine removed and replaced by a small Grenade launcher. Adopted by the U.S. military as a squad heavy support weapon—it is not hard to see why. Use the tests to get used to the Grenade trajectory.

⭐	GOAL SCORE:	450
	TIME LIMIT:	2m 0s

TARGET CHARACTERISTICS: Left/Right

⭐	GOAL TARGETS:	9
	TIME LIMIT:	2m 0s
	AMMO LIMIT:	Bullets-9
		Grenades-9

TARGET CHARACTERISTICS: Flip

NOTES: Lob Grenades when the targets flip around. Aim higher for the targets that appear farther away.

⭐	GOAL TARGETS:	5
	TIME LIMIT:	30s
	AMMO LIMIT:	Bullets-60
		Grenades-4

TARGET CHARACTERISTICS: Middle target—Stationary; others Flip/Pattern

NOTES: If you're good you can take out the closest pair of targets by shooting a Grenade between them. Repeat with the back two targets

SHOTGUN

Subtlety is not an option here. There are two modes, single or double blast. The magazine is quite large for a Shotgun, but be aware of the long reload times and plan your movements accordingly.

GOAL SCORE:	240
TIME LIMIT:	2m 0s

TARGET CHARACTERISTICS: Stationary Pattern

GOAL TARGETS:	9
TIME LIMIT:	30s

TARGET CHARACTERISTICS: Flip; Left/Right
NOTES: Use double-blast, lead the targets a bit, and be sure to follow through with the Shotgun.

GOAL SCORE:	170
TIME LIMIT:	20s
AMMO LIMIT:	30

TARGET CHARACTERISTICS: Left/Right Pattern
NOTES: Use double-blast, lead the target a bit, and be sure to follow through with the Shotgun.

REAPER

Try to control this weapon as best you can. It was designed for a far stronger user than a human, that much is certain. Kneeling down may help steady your aim, but not refine it. If any opponents do make it past the hail of fire, then the barrels can be used as a grinder to inflict damage.

GOAL SCORE:	1000
TIME LIMIT:	2m 0s

TARGET CHARACTERISTICS: Flip
NOTES: Concentrate on one target until it is destroyed. You can do this by kneeling down and not firing when the targets are turned around. Time your reloading when the targets flip over. This will save you time.

GOAL SCORE:	18
TIME LIMIT:	30s

TARGET CHARACTERISTICS: Pattern
NOTES: Kneeling down while using Aiming mode will grant you victory.

GOAL SCORE:	750
GOAL TARGETS:	1
TIME LIMIT:	30s

TARGET CHARACTERISTICS: Right/Left
NOTES: Go to the right of the kiosk and double crouch. Aim for the right target and let the fun begin. Track your fire as the target goes away from you and then go to the targets preceding it.

SNIPER RIFLE

A finely engineered, silenced Sniper Rifle with a high-powered zoom. The only part of the operation that can interfere with the accuracy of the weapon is the sniper. Make sure you use the secondary mode to crouch down and steady your aim.

GOAL SCORE:	120
TIME LIMIT:	2m 0s

TARGET CHARACTERISTICS: Stationary

GOAL SCORE:	120
MIN. ACCURACY:	90%
TIME LIMIT:	2m 0s

TARGET CHARACTERISTICS: Flip; as far targets are destroyed, new targets pop up closer.
NOTES: Sink eight shots into the center of the left target, then keep putting shots into the center of the closer targets as they appear.

GOAL SCORE:	150
TIME LIMIT:	12s
AMMO LIMIT:	15

TARGET CHARACTERISTICS: Back/Forth Pattern
NOTES: Five shots per target; need all bull's-eyes. Line up with center target. Drop five shots into the bull's-eye as it moves away from you. Immediately move left and drop five shots into that target as it approaches you or goes away. Move to the right target and hit the last five bull's-eyes.

FARSIGHT XR-20

Even though the engineering techniques are beyond us, we can still appreciate the effects of the FarSight rifle. The shot is almost unstoppable, and the scope can penetrate walls to a great depth, locking onto targets if need be.

| GOAL TARGETS: | 3 |
| TIME LIMIT: | 2m 0s |

TARGET CHARACTERISTICS: Stationary

| GOAL TARGETS: | 6 |
| TIME LIMIT: | 15s |

TARGET CHARACTERISTICS: Flip; first three act as shields

NOTES: Use the Target Locator mode to locate and destroy the six necessary targets.

GOAL SCORE:	40
GOAL TARGETS:	6
TIME LIMIT:	20s
AMMO LIMIT:	3

TARGET CHARACTERISTICS: Stationary; one target moves Left/Right in second to last row

NOTES: Line up with left target. Use Target Locator. When the moving target is behind the left target, put a shell through the center of all three targets. Move right and destroy the middle target. You can't use the Target Locator on the last target.

DEVASTATOR

A recent dataDyne product, with interesting technology inside it. The secondary mode activates a magnetic field around the bomb, providing adhesion for a limited amount of time. When a certain amount of time has passed, the field is reversed and the bomb falls from the impact point and explodes.

| GOAL TARGETS: | 6 |
| TIME LIMIT: | 2m 0s |

TARGET CHARACTERISTICS: Stationary

GOAL TARGETS:	6
TIME LIMIT:	50s
AMMO LIMIT:	10

TARGET CHARACTERISTICS: Pattern

NOTES: When targets come close, lob a wall hugger. The target will carry the explosive back to blow up the targets farther back. Be careful not to blow up the moving targets with missed wall-hugger shots.

GOAL SCORE:	6
TIME LIMIT:	30s
AMMO LIMIT:	6

TARGET CHARACTERISTICS: Flip

NOTES: Six targets; six wall huggers. It takes lots of practice to hit the correct lobbing angle just as the target has turned around. Using regular Grenades works as well. Just work on the angle; aim higher for targets that are farther away.

ROCKET LAUNCHER

A compact, reusable missile launcher—reload after each shot. The secondary mode uses a variant of the lock-on system from the CMP150 submachine gun, with a single designated target. The missile travels at a slower speed as it tracks the target, so plan for this and time shots carefully.

GOAL TARGETS: 9
TIME LIMIT: 2m 0s

TARGET CHARACTERISTICS: Stationary

GOAL TARGETS: 8
TIME LIMIT: 2m 0s
AMMO LIMIT: 18

TARGET CHARACTERISTICS: Pattern
NOTES: Lock on and fire away.

GOAL SCORE: 40
GOAL TARGETS: 4
TIME LIMIT: 30s
AMMO LIMIT: 4

TARGET CHARACTERISTICS: Flip; Pattern
NOTES: Time rockets to hit targets as they flip toward you.

SLAYER

This Skedar handheld missile launcher can fire either an unguided rocket or a user-controlled remote rocket. Presumably this gave the Skedar some perverse satisfaction when the warhead camera closed on the target, but a Carrington Institute agent is beyond such things. The guided rocket speeds up automatically, but can be slowed down for greater maneuverability. Detonation occurs on contact or when the trigger is pressed.

GOAL TARGETS: 6
TIME LIMIT: 2m 0s

TARGET CHARACTERISTICS: Flip; Pattern
NOTES: Targets can be destroyed when flipped.

GOAL SCORE: 40
GOAL TARGETS: 4
TIME LIMIT: 2m 0s
AMMO LIMIT: 6

TARGET CHARACTERISTICS: Pattern
NOTES: Launch missiles at targets. Use Fly-by-Wire mode if you have trouble.

GOAL SCORE: 60
GOAL TARGETS: 6
TIME LIMIT: 40s
AMMO LIMIT: 8

TARGET CHARACTERISTICS: Flip; Pattern
NOTES: Use Fly-by-Wire mode. Only front-facing targets will explode. Sometimes the target will flip in the explosion and be destroyed.

COMBAT KNIFE

A finely tempered fighting knife, which is also balanced for throwing. Practice is essential to get accustomed to the range and trajectory of the thrown blade. Holding [Z] cocks your arm and helps a bit with accuracy and timing your throw.

GOAL SCORE: 72
TIME LIMIT: 2m 0s

TARGET CHARACTERISTICS: Stationary

GOAL SCORE: 90
TIME LIMIT: 2m 0s
AMMO LIMIT: 18

TARGET CHARACTERISTICS: Flip
NOTES: Take your time and hit the center of targets.

GOAL SCORE: 80
GOAL TARGETS: 8
TIME LIMIT: 30s

TARGET CHARACTERISTICS: Pattern
NOTES: Must hit eight bull's-eyes. Line up on the right or the left and wait for each target to stop in front of you, then throw.

CROSSBOW

The primary function of the Crossbow is a nonlethal drugged shot, while the secondary is an instant kill. It is a stealth weapon first and foremost, so the reloading can be time-consuming and inconvenient in a firefight.

	★		★		★
Goal Score:	72	Goal Score:	90	Goal Score:	150
Time Limit:	2m 0s	Time Limit:	2m 0s	Time Limit:	30s
		Ammo Limit:	20		

Target Characteristics: Stationary

Target Characteristics: Stationary

Notes: Hit nine bull's-eyes. Best to hit three bull's-eyes in three different targets. Too many arrows seem to clog up the bull's-eye and deny points.

Target Characteristics: Flip; Left/Right

Notes: Must hit 15 bull's-eyes in 30 seconds. Simply line up with the target and stay in one spot, shooting only when the targets appear in front of you. You can generally get three to four shots in before the target flips. It's important not to waste ammo due to the slow reload time of the Crossbow.

TRANQUILIZER

The Tranquilizer gun is a common design, found in many medical laboratories and hospitals worldwide. It can be switched from the Tranquilizer pellets to a short-range lethal dose, which uses up a lot more of the reservoir of sedative.

	★		★		★
Goal Score:	120	Goal Score:	250	Goal Score:	18
Time Limit:	2m 0s	Time Limit:	20s	Time Limit:	15s
				Ammo Limit:	18

Target Characteristics: Pattern

Target Characteristics: Flip

Notes: Reload while targets are flipped. Don't waste ammo; put all shots into the bull's-eye. Any misses severely hamper your chances for passing this test.

Target Characteristics: Pattern

Notes: One shot; one kill. You must be *fast, fast, fast* and learn the pattern. Have your Tranquilizer gun already pointed to where the next target pops up.

LASER

The experimental weapons department has come up with a small but effective wrist-mounted Laser with two beam settings. The primary mode fires a blast out to a considerable range, while the secondary mode provides a continual beam for as long as the trigger is pressed. Use of the secondary weapon garners no points in the training exercises.

GOAL SCORE:	250
TIME LIMIT:	2m 0s

TARGET CHARACTERISTICS: Stationary

GOAL SCORE:	180
MIN. ACCURACY:	80%
TIME LIMIT:	20s

TARGET CHARACTERISTICS: Left/Right; Flip

NOTES: Line up with the target to the right. As the target moves, strafe and lead your fire. You will be able to get in four to five shots.

GOAL SCORE:	250
MIN. ACCURACY:	100%
TIME LIMIT:	20s

TARGET CHARACTERISTICS: Back/Forth

NOTES: Each target takes twelve shots to be destroyed. Make them count. Remember to make sure that you do not miss the targets or it's game over.

GRENADE

The fragmentation anti-personnel Grenade has four seconds from activation to detonation on the basic fuse. For your entertainment and delight, we have included a secondary mode—Proximity Pinball. The Grenade will bounce around until the charge wears off or the proximity detector is triggered.

GOAL TARGETS:	3
TIME LIMIT:	2m 0s

TARGET CHARACTERISTICS: Stationary

GOAL TARGETS:	18
TIME LIMIT:	30s

TARGET CHARACTERISTICS: Stationary

NOTES: Stand to the extreme right. Throw a Grenade in the center of the back row, then one in the front row. Wait for the explosion to die down, then repeat. watch out for holes in the floor.

GOAL TARGETS:	4
TIME LIMIT:	30s
AMMO LIMIT:	6

TARGET CHARACTERISTICS: Flip; Pattern

NOTES: Use Proximity Pinball for all targets, angling off the last two walls.

TIMED MINE

A degree of judgment is required for effective use of Timed Mines, otherwise the intended target may overrun the explosion range and come after you. Hone your skills in the tests before you make a critical error in the field. The secondary function is a Threat Detector identical to that found on the K7 Avenger Assault Rifle.

GOAL TARGETS:	3
TIME LIMIT:	2m0s

TARGET CHARACTERISTICS: Flip

GOAL TARGETS:	6
TIME LIMIT:	2m 0s
AMMO LIMIT:	6

TARGET CHARACTERISTICS: Back/Forth Pattern

NOTES: Throw mines out to targets; they will break.

GOAL SCORE:	60
GOAL TARGETS:	6
TIME LIMIT:	12s
AMMO LIMIT:	1

TARGET CHARACTERISTICS: Back/Forth Pattern

NOTES: Throw the mine into the center of the targets. The blast radius destroys all six targets if timed correctly.

PROXIMITY MINE

The key to successful placement of Proximity Mines is to put them where your opponent doesn't expect to encounter them. If you find yourself on the receiving end of Proximity Mines, use the Threat Detector secondary mode to make sure of your surroundings. It may be wasting your time, but it could save your life.

	GOAL TARGETS:	3
★	TIME LIMIT:	2n 0s

TARGET CHARACTERISTICS: Stationary

	GOAL TARGETS:	3
★	TIME LIMIT:	2n 0s
	AMMO LIMIT:	6

TARGET CHARACTERISTICS: Back/Forth Pattern

NOTES: Throw the mines so they attach to targets. When targets move past each other, they blow up.

	GOAL TARGETS:	5
★	TIME LIMIT:	30s
	AMMO LIMIT:	4

TARGET CHARACTERISTICS: Flip; Left/Right Pattern; Back/Forth Pattern

NOTES: Throw mines near targets (best if you can attach them). You can blow up targets even if mines are attached to the back of the target.

REMOTE MINE

The latest variety of remote detonated mines, they're essentially the same as all that have gone before. The primary mode is placing the mines, while the secondary mode is giving the detonation command. If you can't see the mine, you'll have to rely on old-fashioned guesswork and timing.

	GOAL TARGETS:	3
★	TIME LIMIT:	2n 0s

TARGET CHARACTERISTICS: Stationary

	GOAL TARGETS:	4
★	TIME LIMIT:	2n 0s
	AMMO LIMIT:	4

TARGET CHARACTERISTICS: Flip; Pattern

NOTES: Use the Ⓐ and Ⓑ trick to throw the Remote Mine between the targets and detonate them in the air.

	GOAL TARGETS:	7
★	TIME LIMIT:	12s
	AMMO LIMIT:	2

TARGET CHARACTERISTICS: Left/Right Pattern (center target Stationary)

NOTES: Attach a mine to center target. Move to the left and throw the other mine to attach it to the back left target. Detonate as targets move past each other.

holotraining

Holo 1—Looking Around

Examine all of the objects by looking directly at them. Facing the terminals along the wall, they are numbered left to right 1 through 4. Code 1 is along the upper right wall. Code 2 is on the floor along the left wall. Codes 3 and 4 are on the ceiling toward the back of the room.

For greater precision and freedom when looking around, use the Aiming mode.

THE CARRINGTON INSTITUTE

Holo 2—Movement 1

Activate all of the switches in front. Be quick, though, as each switch will reset on a time limit. Strafe (©◄ and ©►) along the bank of terminals, stopping just long enough to activate each one.

 Sidestepping and strafing can get you out of trouble.

Holo 3—Movement 2

Work your way through the obstacles using the moves available to you. Activate the switches. Duck underneath the lasers and activate all the switches.

 Ducking enables you to reach places normally inaccessible to you, but remember that you move quickest when standing upright. Duck only when you have to.

Holo 4—Unarmed Combat 1

Knock out all enemies without getting hit. Flail away at these dorks until they are knocked out. It helps to circle-strafe while punching to avoid being the recipient of a cheap shot.

 Attacking from behind may be dishonorable, but doing so makes it easier to take them down. Close only to fighting distance when you have to, and be prepared to step back out of range when enemies attack you.

 For exercises 5 and 7, stealth is the key. Hide behind the wall until enemies forget you're in the room, then get behind them to deliver a love tap that puts their lights out.

Holo 5—Unarmed Combat 2

Knock out/disarm all enemies without getting hit. The last guard on this holo mission can be a little tricky to defeat; he is a crack shot and it's one shot, one kill. Disarm the first guard and knock him out. Hide behind the wall to the far side of the room from where the second guard spawns. You want to bait him. He will walk to your position. Loop around the wall and you will be behind him. Take him out. Be prepared to deal with the final guard, who will spawn close to that end of the wall. Circle-strafe and punch the final guard into submission. It takes at least three shots to the dome to put him down.

Holo 6—Live Combat 1

Beat all the unarmed enemies without getting hit. Another rock 'em, sock 'em connection. Beat down all comers.

 Don't hang around and wait to get hit; move! Don't focus on one opponent; try to be aware of where all of them are. If you can't see all of them, move until you can.

Holo 7—Live Combat 2

Beat all the armed enemies without getting hit. You start this exercise right in the line of fire, and, once again, it's one shot, one kill. Immediately head forward and veer right, circling around the guard to the right. Run past him and the next guard. Disarm the third guard (quickly now), and take cover behind the wall. Be prepared to take out the three unarmed guards who will come busting in after you. Two are the unarmed guards who start the level and the third is the sucker you disarmed. Don't let them get in a cheap shot that will ruin your run.

Three down; two to go. Head to the end of the wall farthest from the remaining guards. Don't peek out unless you want to get shot in the face. Take a deep breath and strafe, bob, and weave until *only you* are left standing.

 Go for the armed opponents once you are confident of your hand-to-hand skills. Back away from the disarmed enemies and use their weapons on them before they get too close to you.

There's not a whole lot to be found in the Hangar when you start the game (you'll revisit this level in the solo missions). You can get some practice in on the HoverBike if you choose the door to the right. The door to the far left leads to a surly gentleman who has a computer with info on locations and vehicles you may run into.

 Double-tap ® to get on/off the HoverBike.

Challenges

So, are you confident that no enemy poses a threat to you? Think you have a grasp of the secret agent job?

Well, you're wrong. To be Perfect, you have to practice, practice, practice. The Combat Simulator lets you hone your skills against computer opponents—Simulants—either by yourself or with a few human friends.

To pit your skills against the Challenges, select "Combat Simulator" in the Perfect menu. Highlight "Challenges" in the next menu and you're ready to choose.

You can play a Challenge with one to four people. It will be players versus Simulants in all Challenges—even straight Combat Scenarios.

You'll earn a gold star every time you complete a Challenge—*without* any cheats enabled. You can earn a total of four stars in each Challenge. Complete it with one player and you'll earn the first star. Complete it with two players to get the second star, and so on.

When you earn your first star in a Challenge—with however many players—a new Challenge will open up. There are a total of 30 Challenges. And yes, in case you were wondering, the Challenges get harder as you go.

Much harder.

Four Challenges to begin with. Don't worry, there are plenty more.

Challenge 1 has been completed with two and three players, Challenge 2 with one, two, three, and four players, and Challenge 3 with only one player.

NOTE

The list of Simulants for each Challenge is color coded. The blue ones appear on all levels—one through four players. Red appear in two-through four-player Challenges, green in three- through four-player Challenges, and yellow only in four-player Challenges.

How to Read the Information

sample challenge ☐☐☐☐☐☐

COMBAT: Here you'll find what type of Challenge it is and the description given in the *Perfect Dark* game.

The weapons and devices available in the Challenge.

Weapons

Falcon 2
Cyclone
FarSight XR-20

Simulants

GuardSim: 1— Meat
GuardSim: 2— Easy, Hard
GuardSim: 3— Normal
GuardSim: 4— Normal

A list of the Simulants you'll combat and their Difficulty. They're color coded to show when they appear.

ONE PLAYER AND ABOVE
TWO PLAYERS AND ABOVE
THREE PLAYERS AND ABOVE
FOUR PLAYERS

The Difficulty level can change with the number of players. Here GuardSim: 2 is Easy with two players but Hard with three players.

ARENA: This tells you what map you're playing on.

LIMITS: 10 minutes or Team Score: 1P—10, 2P—20, 3P—25, 4P—30

If the time limit or Team Score is met the Challenge will end. The Team Score can change with the number of players, but it doesn't always. Here the one-player game limit is 10 points and the two-player game limit is 20 points.

Here you'll find advice and/or encouragement specific to the Challenge.

TIPS Unlocking certain Challenges (just unlocking them—you don't have to beat them or even play them) will open up new options in the multiplayer menus, allowing further customization.

The circled letters (**A**) show where the different floors connect. They indicate stairs, ramps, elevators, even holes in the ground. Each map also shows where items and weapons spawn (🔫). Where a specific weapon—such as a Falcon 2—appears depends on which slot it occupies in the Weapons Set. Study the item spots so you can find the tools you need in a hurry.

challenge 1 ☐☐☐☐☐☐

Combat: A Challenge against basic Simulants using standard weaponry.

Weapons

Falcon 2
CMP150
Sniper Rifle
DY357 Magnum
Dragon

Simulants

ShockSim:1—■ Meat
GuardSim:1—■ Meat

Arena: Skedar

Limits: Five minutes or Team Score: 1P—4, 2P—8, 3P—10, 4P—12

This is a basic Combat scenario, players against Simulants. With a max of two Simulants—both at Meat Difficulty—you shouldn't have too much trouble with this one. Don't shoot your teammates (if you have any) and get to know the map.

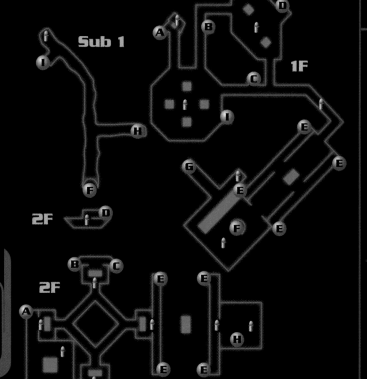

Skedar

challenge 2 ☐☐☐☐☐☐

Combat: A Challenge against basic Simulants that includes the use of Rocket Launchers.

Weapons

Combat Knife
Falcon 2
Cyclone
Dragon
Rocket Launcher

Simulants

ShockSim:1—■ Meat
GuardSim:1—■ Meat
ShockSim:2—■ Meat

Arena: Area 52

Limits: Five minutes or Team Score: 1P—6, 2P—12, 3P—15, 4P—18

Not much different from Challenge 1, but with the addition of Rocket Launchers it's much easier to hurt yourself or teammates. Know the map and know the damage range of those rockets.

Area 52

challenge 3 ☐☐☐☐☐☐

Combat: A Challenge against basic Simulants that includes Assault Rifles and Timed Mines.

Weapons
MagSec 4
CMP150
Timed Mine
Dragon
AR34

Simulants
TechSim:1— ▪ Meat
TechSim:2— ▪ Meat
TechSim:3— ▪ Meat
TechSim:4— ▪ Meat

Arena: Pipes

Limits: Five minutes or Team Score: 1P—8, 2P—16, 3P—20, 4P—24

The Timed Mines are fun. If you manage to stick one directly on an opponent, you're guaranteed to score. Once again, be careful of the splash damage the mines cause. You can hurt yourself.

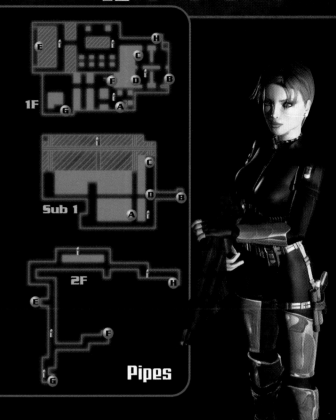

Pipes

challenge 4 ☐☐☐☐☐☐

King of the Hill: Take control of the hill against a team of standard Simulants. Shield technology is available, as well as the K7 Avenger.

Weapons
MagSec 4
CMP150
Dragon
K7 Avenger
Shield

Simulants
CISim:1— ▪ Easy
CISim:2— ▪ Meat, ▪ Easy
CISim:3— ▪ Meat

Arena: Skedar

Limits: 10 minutes or Team Score: 1P—4, 2P—8, 3P—10, 4P—12

This King of the Hill Challenge has few surprises. Grab the hill and defend it. The Shields are of little consequence with these low-level Simulants, but in later Challenges, you'll see them used constantly.

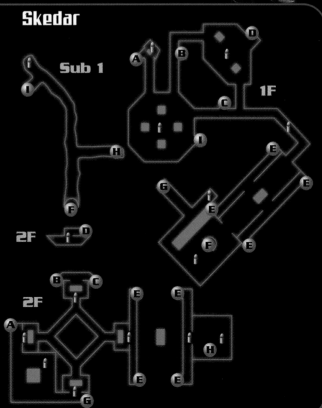

Skedar

challenge 5 □□□□□□

COMBAT: Combat a team of standard Simulants using the specialized FarSight weapon in the Complex.

Weapons

Cyclone
Grenade
AR34
FarSight XR-20
Shield

Simulants

CassSim— ■ Easy
GuardSim:1— ■ Meat, ■ Easy
GuardSim:2— ■ Meat

ARENA: Complex

LIMITS: 10 minutes or Team Score: 1P—10, 2P—20, 3P—25, 4P—30

The FarSight gun can be excellent fun. Use the Target Locator function and pick off opponents through walls. Careful, though; if someone stumbles on you while you're aiming, you're a sitting duck.

Unlocking Challenge 5 also makes the Complex Arena available for multiplayer games.

Complex

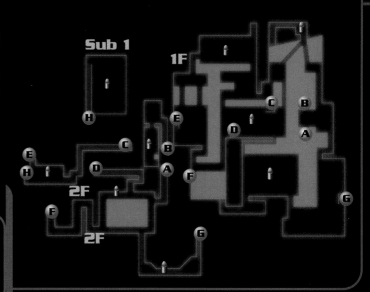

challenge 6 □□□□□□

HOLD THE BRIEFCASE: Hold the briefcase for as long as possible against a large team of basic Simulants.

Weapons

CMP150
DY357 Magnum
Shotgun
K7 Avenger
Shield

Simulants

WorkSim:1— ■ Meat, ■ Easy
WorkSim:2— ■ Meat, ■ Easy
WorkSim:3— ■ Meat
WorkSim:4— ■ Meat

ARENA: Area 52

LIMITS: 10 minutes or Team Score 6

When playing single-player, get the briefcase and then get into a room with a rolling door. The Simulants will come in the door and right into your gunfire. With multiple players, try the same strategy, one player with the briefcase and the others standing guard.

Once Challenge 6 is available, you can play Hold the Briefcase Scenarios in multiplayer.

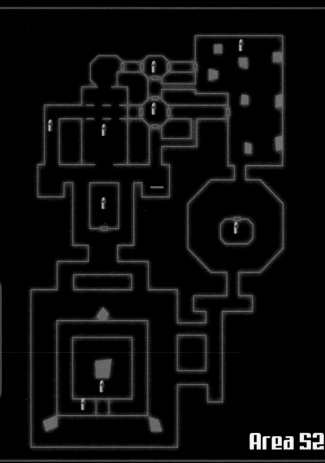

Area 52

PERFECT DARK™

challenge 7 ☐☐☐☐☐☐

KING OF THE HILL: Take control of the hill against a team of advanced Simulants in the Warehouse. All weapons kill with only one hit.

Weapons
Falcon 2 (silencer)
MagSec 4
Cyclone
Grenade
Shield

Simulants
JoSim:1 — ■ Easy
JoSim:2 — ■ Meat, ■ Easy

ARENA: Warehouse

LIMITS: 10 minutes or Team Score: 1P—5, 2P—10, 3P—12, 4P—15

This Challenge will be easy if you know the map well. Getting to the hills quickly will usually guarantee a capture. The one-hit-kill rule makes the MagSec 4 and the Cyclone the preferable choices.

Opening Challenge 7—you don't have to play it, just open it up—will open "One-Hit Kills" in the Game Setup Options menu. You can select it when creating your own multiplayer games.

When Challenge 7 is opened, the Warehouse Arena is unlocked in multiplayer.

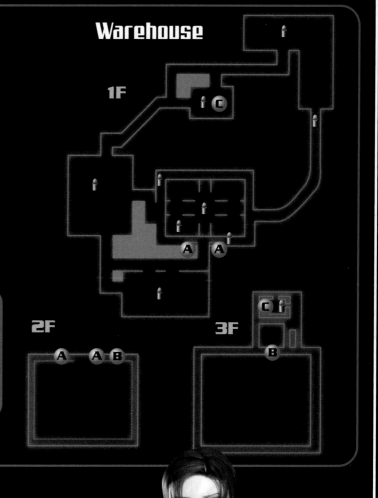

Warehouse

1F

2F

3F

PERFECT DARK™

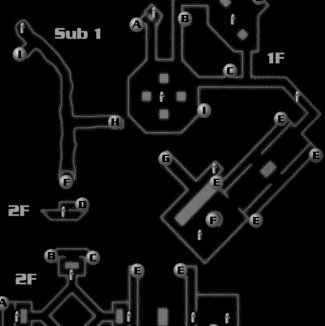

Skedar

Sub 1

1F

2F

2F

challenge 8 ⬜⬜⬜⬜⬜⬜

COMBAT: Capture the Case: Capture the enemy's case while defending your own. Killing the case carrier means the case returns to the base.

Weapons

MagSec 4
K7 Avenger
Shotgun
SuperDragon
Shield

Simulants

SnipeSim:1— ⬜ Easy
SnipeSim:2— ⬜ Easy
SnipeSim:3— ⬛ Meat
SnipeSim:4— ◨ Meat

ARENA: Skedar

LIMITS: 10 minutes or Team Score 9

Guess what? A tie game is a win for you. If these guys give you too much trouble—though they probably won't—guard your case and don't let the Simulants score. It's a cheap win, but it's still a win.

When Challenge 8 is opened, the Capture the Case Scenario is unlocked for multiplayer.

Ravine

3F

2F

2F

3F

4F

5F

1F

challenge 9 ⬜⬜⬜⬜⬜⬜

COMBAT: A one-hit-kill scenario against expert Simulants. Weapons include the FarSight and the Laptop Gun.

Weapons

Falcon 2
DY357 Magnum
Timed Mine
Laptop Gun
FarSight XR-20

Simulants

TrentSim— ⬛ Normal
NSASim:1— ⬛ Meat, ⬜ Easy

ARENA: Ravine

LIMITS: 10 minutes or Team Score: 1P—10, 2P—20, 3P—25, 4P—30

Once again the one-hit-kill rule makes the automatic weapons very valuable. However, the FarSight is also a good weapon to have. Use the Laptop Gun's secondary mode—the Sentry Gun—to grab some quick points.

Opening Challenge 9 also opens the Ravine Arena for your multiplayer games.

CHALLENGES

challenge 10 □□□□□□

HACKER CENTRAL: Fight against a team of Simulants to hack the terminal using the Data Uplink.

Weapons
CMP150
Cyclone
Remote Mine
AR34
Shield

Simulants
GuardSim:1— ☐ Easy, ☐ Normal
SWATSim:1— ☐ Easy, ☐ Normal
GuardSim:2— ☐ Easy

ARENA: Temple

LIMITS: 10 minutes or Team Score 3

This is another game where a tie means success for you. The Simulants aren't too hard, and they're not very bright. Keep control of either the Data Uplink or the terminal and you'll walk away a winner. With multiple players, designate a person to find the Uplink and just keep downloading while the others guard.

 Unlocking Challenge 10 will open the Hacker Central Scenario *and* the Temple Arena.

Temple

challenge 11 □□□□□□

KING OF THE HILL: King of the Hill against expert Simulants. Weapons include the Shotgun and Tranquilizer.

Weapons
MagSec 4
Tranquilizer
Shotgun
K7 Avenger
Shield

Simulants
BlondeSim:1— ☐ Normal
BlondeSim:2— ☐ Normal
BlondeSim:3— ☐ Hard
BlondeSim:4— ☐ Hard

ARENA: Complex

LIMITS: 10 minutes or Team Score 10

With only one Simulant to deal with, this Challenge will fall to your skills easily, right? The BlondeSim is quick and canny, so you need to get the advantage early and keep it. With several players, send one to the hill, one to help guard, and the others—if any—to seek and destroy the Simulant.

 Unlocking Challenge 11 makes HardSim and the Tranquilizer Weapons Set available for multiplayer games. Also, you can now pack eight Simulants into a multiplayer game instead of just four.

Complex

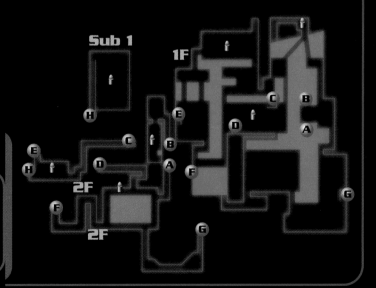

challenge 12 ☐☐☐☐☐☐

Skedar

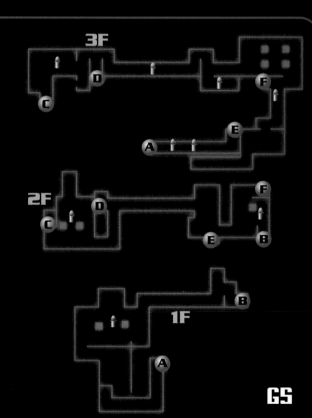

COMBAT: Slow-motion combat in the Skedar Arena.

Weapons
Falcon 2 (scope)
Sniper Rifle
Shotgun
SuperDragon
Shield

Simulants
JoSim:1— Hard
JoSim:2— Normal
JoSim:3— ☐ Easy
JoSim:4— ☐ Easy

ARENA: Skedar

LIMITS: 10 minutes or Team Score: 1P—3, 2P—6, 3P—7, 4P—9

Slow-motion combat is a blast. Use the effect to your advantage by placing your shots carefully. Watch out for SuperDragon Grenades. With one player, find a weapon and then wait for the Simulant to come to you.

TIPS Opening Challenge 12 will unlock "Slow Motion" in the Game Setup Options menu for use in your multiplayer games.

---

challenge 13 ☐☐☐☐☐☐

COMBAT: One-hit kills in the G5 building with Tranquilizers.

Weapons
Falcon 2 (silencer)
Tranquilizer
Laptop Gun
Grenade
Reaper

Simulants
CIASim:1— Normal, Hard
FBISim:1— Easy
CIASim:2— ☐ Easy
FBISim:2— ☐ Easy

ARENA: G5 Building

LIMITS: 10 minutes or Team Score: 1P—10, 2P—20, 3P—25, 4P—30

The cheap and easy way to win is the Laptop Gun. Deploy it as a Sentry Gun in a secure area and you're set. A good spot to deploy is the walkway in the biggest open room. Let the Simulants walk into the withering fire and watch your score climb.

Once Challenge 13 is opened, the G5 Building will be open in the Arenas menu for multiplayer.

PERFECT DARK™

challenge 14 □□□□□

CAPTURE THE CASE: Capture the case in Area 52 with cloaking.

Weapons

Cyclone
SuperDragon
K7 Avenger
FarSight XR-20
Cloaking Device

Simulants

GuardSim:1— □ Normal, ■ Hard
TroopSim:1— □ Easy, ■ Normal
GuardSim:2— □ Easy
AirSim:1— □ Easy
GuardSim:3— ■ Easy
TroopSim:2— ▨ Easy

ARENA: Area 52

LIMITS: 10 minutes or Team Score 10

Once again a tie will win it for you. With one player, run for the opponents' case and capture it at least once. You can then play it safe and sit tight in your base, guarding, or rush for the case twice more to end the game when you hit three points.

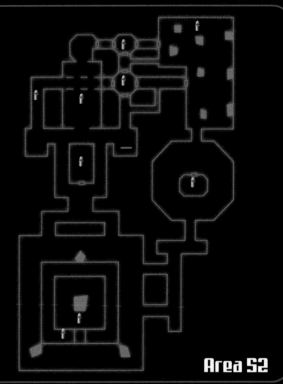

Area 52

challenge 15 □□□□□

HOLD THE BRIEFCASE: Hold the Briefcase in the Grid with Devastators.

Weapons

MagSec4
Dragon
Shotgun
Devastator
Shield

Simulants

LabSim:1— ■ Normal, □ Hard
LabSim:2— □ Meat, □ Normal
LabSim:3— □ Meat, ■ Easy
LabSim:4— ■ Meat, ▨ Easy
LabSim:5— ■ Meat

ARENA: Grid

LIMITS: 10 minutes or Team Score 10

Get the briefcase first. That's important. Arm yourself well and then hole up. Stay in a defensible spot and the Simulants will usually run themselves ragged trying to get you. If there are multiple players, have them guard the case carrier in a secure spot. If the player(s) control one or both of the areas where the Devastator spawns, they will have a significant advantage over the Sims.

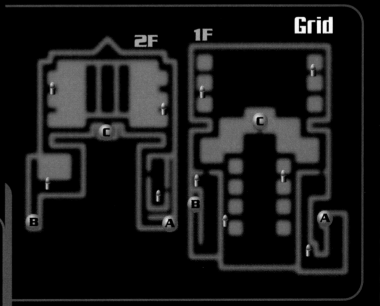

Grid

2F   1F

Opening Challenge 15 will also open the Grid Arena plus the Explosive *and* Grenade Launcher Weapons Sets in multiplayer.

challenge 16 □□□□□□

COMBAT: Standard combat. Weapons include Proximity Mines. There is no radar on this Challenge.

Weapons

Falcon 2
K7 Avenger
SuperDragon
Proximity Mine
Shield

Simulants

BioSim:1— ■ Perfect
BioSim:2— ■ Normal, ■ Hard
BioSim:3— ■ Meat, ■ Easy
BioSim:4— ■ Easy

ARENA: Felicity

LIMITS: 10 minutes or Team Score: 1P—10, 2P—20, 3P—25, 4P—30

This one is the beginning of the truly difficult Challenges. The lack of radar will hamper you because you can't see how close your enemies are to shooting you. The Simulants are aggressive and they will always know where you are. Blast them enough to get ahead, then hole up and lay some Proximity Mines to keep them at bay for a cheap win.

TIPS Unlocking Challenge 16 also unlocks the PerfectSim, Felicity Arena, Proximity Mine Weapons Set, and Pop a Cap Scenario for use in multiplayer games.

Felicity

challenge 17 □□□□□□

KING OF THE HILL: A King of the Hill game. Weapons include Fly-by-Wire Missles.

Weapons

DY357 Magnum
AR34
Reaper
Slayer
Shield

Simulants

DanSim— ■ Perfect, ■ Hard, ■ Perfect
CISim:1— ■ Easy, ■ Normal
CISim:2— ■ Meat, ■ Easy
CISim:3— ■ Meat (doesn't appear in 3P game)

ARENA: Temple

LIMITS: 10 minutes or Team Score: 1P—10, 2P—20, 3P—25, 4P—30

The Fly-by-Wire Missles—launched from the Slayer—sound good in theory but you can't see the radar while you guide one of the rockets. The Simulants don't seem to have that trouble and use the Slayer with deadly accuracy. In multi-player games, try to control the areas where the Slayer appears as well as the hill. It's difficult, but worth it.

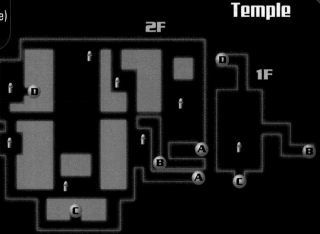

Temple

CHALLENGES (vertical, left margin)

54

challenge 18 □□□□□□

KING OF THE HILL: A King of the Hill game against a team of expert Simulants.

Weapons

Falcon 2
Phoenix
Tranquilizer
Laptop Gun
Shield
Cloaking Device

Simulants

ElvisSim— ■ Perfect, ■ Normal
MaianSim:1— ■ Meat, ■ Hard, ■ Normal
MaianSim:2— ■ Meat, ■ Easy
MaianSim:3— ■ Easy
MaianSim:4— ■ Meat
MaianSim:5— ■ Meat

ARENA: Villa

LIMITS: 10 minutes or Team Score: 1P—10, 2P—20, 3P—25, 4P—30

Not only are the Simulants very hard to beat, they're also short. Laptop Guns will again be useful as Sentry Guns. You *need* Shields and Cloaking Devices. Your opponents will use them to frustrating effect. Make sure you know this map very well or you'll get beat silly.

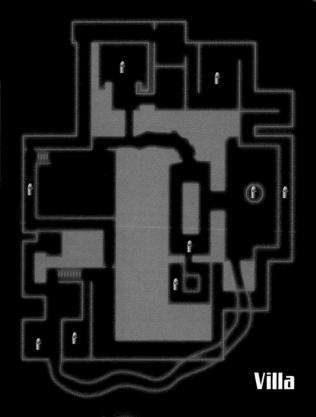

Villa

When Challenge 18 is opened, the Villa Arena will be available in multiplayer.

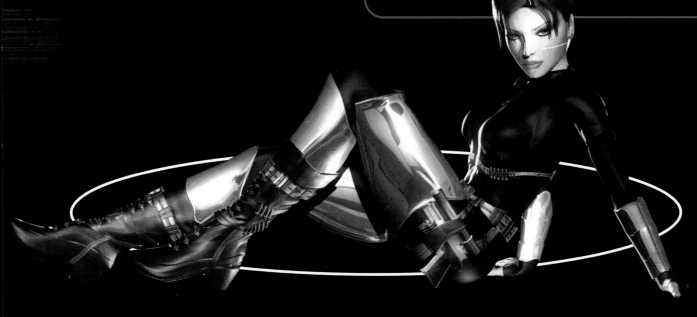

challenge 19 ⬚⬚⬚⬚⬚⬚

COMBAT: Fast movement combat against expert Simulants. Weapons include the Rocket Launcher and the FarSight.

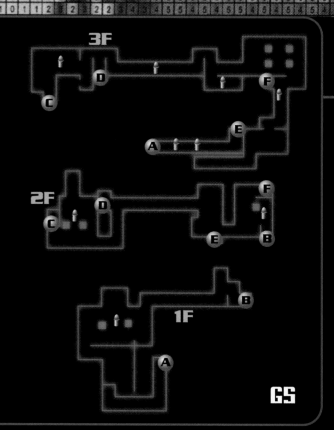

3F

2F

1F

GS

Weapons

- CMP150
- Shotgun
- Rocket Launcher
- FarSight XR-20
- Shield
- Combat Boost

Simulants

CassSim— ⬚ Hard, ⬚ Perfect
TrentSim— ⬚ Easy, ⬚ Perfect, ⬚ Hard
SnipeSim:1— ⬚ Normal
SnipeSim:2— ⬚ Easy

ARENA: G5 Building

LIMITS: 10 minutes or Team Score: 1P—10, 2P—20, 3P—25, 4P—30

Choosing your ground and weapons are key to winning this Challenge. The best spot—especially for one player—is in the dead-end walkway where you find a Shotgun. Collect a FarSight and a Rocket Launcher and then camp out in that area. Use the FarSight to pick off enemies and the Rocket Launcher to keep them at bay if they get too close.

---

challenge 20 ⬚⬚⬚⬚⬚⬚

COMBAT: One-hit-kill combat with a twist—protect the weaker Simulants on your team. Weapons include pistols and Shields.

Sewers

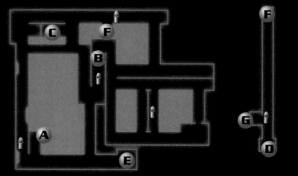

Mid Levels

Top Levels

Sub Levels

Weapons

- Mauler
- Falcon 2
- MagSec 4
- DY357 Magnum
- Shield

Simulants

PilotSim:1— ⬚ Hard, ⬚ Perfect
Pilot Sim:2— ⬚ Hard, ⬚ Perfect
AirSim:1— ⬚ Normal (on your team)
AirSim:2— ⬚ Normal (on your team)
AirSim:3— ⬚ Normal (on your team)

ARENA: Sewers

LIMITS: 10 minutes or Team Score: 1P—10, 2P—20, 3P—25, 4P—30

Know the map like the back of your hand. The opponent's Simulant is fast and will tear up your Simulants—and you, at first. Stick close to your Sims and protect them. Grab Shields and hunt the Yellow Team down.

Once Challenge 20 is open, you can select the Sewers Arena and the Heavy Weapons Set in multiplayer.

CHALLENGES

PERFECT DARK™

challenge 21 □□□□□□

HACKER CENTRAL: Hack into the terminal using the Data Uplink. The Cloaking Device is available.

Weapons
- Mauler
- Reaper
- Shotgun
- Callisto NTG
- Cloaking Device

Simulants
- JoSim— ■ Hard
- SnowSim:1— ■ Normal
- SnowSim:2— ■ Easy, ■ Normal
- SnowSim:3— ■ Easy

ARENA: Grid

LIMITS: 10 minutes or Team Score 10

Use the Cloaking Device. Grab that Data Uplink, cloak, and then start downloading. Repeat. Once you're ahead of them in points, you can simply grab the Data Uplink and hide or guard the terminal. Make sure to fire a shot every now and then to take care of any cloaked opponents trying to download.

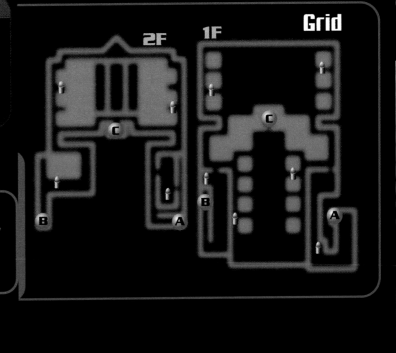

Grid

The Car Park Arena and the FarSight Weapons Set open in multiplayer when Challenge 21 is unlocked.

challenge 22 □□□□□□

HOLD THE BRIEFCASE: A Hold the Briefcase game with one-hit kills. Weapons include the Crossbow and the Sniper Rifle.

Weapons
- Falcon 2
- Sniper Rifle
- Crossbow
- K7 Avenger
- Shield

Simulants
- PresSim— ■ Perfect
- GuardSim:1— ■ Normal, ■ Hard, ■ Normal
- GuardSim:2— ■ Easy, ■ Normal
- GuardSim:3— ■ Easy

ARENA: Base

LIMITS: 10 minutes or Team Score 10

These Simulants will walk all over you if you let them get the case first. Make nabbing the case your top priority and then survive long enough to get into a secure position. Use the radar to your advantage, popping the Simulants just as they round a corner. It's one-hit kills, so stay sharp.

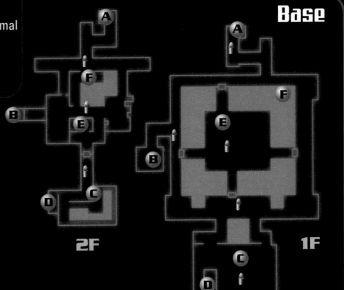

Base

Unlocking Challenge 22 unlocks the Base Arena in multiplayer.

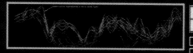

challenge 23 □□□□□□

COMBAT: Combat in slow motion. Weapons include the RC-P120.

Weapons

- MagSec 4
- Grenade
- Laptop Gun
- RC-P120
- Shield
- Combat Boost

Simulants

CloneSim— ■ Hard, ■ Perfect
StripeSim:1— ■ Hard, ■ Perfect
StripeSim:2— ■ Hard, ■ Normal
StripeSim:3— ■ Normal

ARENA: Complex

LIMITS: 10 minutes or Team Score: 1P—2, 2P—4, 3P—5, 4P—6

> Slow motion is always fun. The Laptop Gun is your friend again. Deploy it strategically as a Sentry Gun in one of the many long hallways. Aim carefully—since you have time—and you shouldn't have too much trouble.

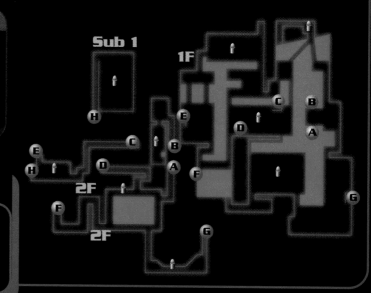

Complex

Sub 1 · 1F · 2F · 2F

challenge 24 □□□□□□

CAPTURE THE CASE: Capture the Case game against a team of expert Simulants. Weapons include the Gold DY357 Magnum and the Tranquilizer.

Weapons

- CMP150
- Tranquilizer
- Devastator
- SuperDragon
- DY357-LX

Simulants

GuardSim:1— ■ Easy, ■ Normal, ■ Hard
TroopSim:1— ■ Easy, ■ Normal, ■ Hard
AirSim:1— ■ Easy, ■ Normal
GuardSim:2— ■ Easy, ■ Normal
TroopSim:2— ■ Easy
AirSim:2— ■ Perfect, ■ Easy

ARENA: Fortress

LIMITS: No time limit, Team Score 9

> No time limit means there's no tie game. You must score nine points to win, so don't just hang around. Rush the base and use the Magnum if you're a good shot—the Devastator if you're not. With multiple players have one person guard the ramp into your case room and another guard the room above with the two roll-up doors.

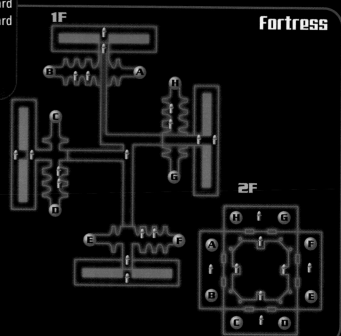

Fortress

1F · 2F

Once Challenge 24 is opened, the Fortress Arena and Golden Magnum Weapons Set will become available in multiplayer.

CHALLENGES

58

challenge 25 ▢▢▢▢▢

COMBAT: A standard combat game with N-Bombs and Cloaking Devices. The Simulant team is composed of experts.

Weapons

Mauler
N-Bomb
K7 Avenger
FarSight XR-20
Cloaking Device

Simulants

ShockSim:1— ▢ Perfect
ShockSim:2— ▢ Hard, ▢ Perfect
ShockSim:3— ▢ Hard, ▢ Perfect
ShockSim:4— ▢ Normal, ▢ Hard
ShockSim:5— ▢ Easy

ARENA: Ravine

LIMITS: Three minutes or Team Score: 1P—10, 2P—20, 3P—25, 4P—30

The N-Bombs make their first appearance here. They're like area-affect sedatives, so don't get caught in the blast. This is a short game; score your points fast. The FarSight is a trustworthy tool for this level, so grab it.

 Once you've seen the N-Bombs, you can select them for a regular multiplayer game.

Ravine

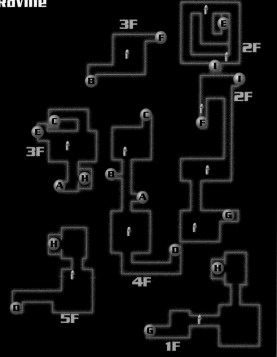

challenge 26 ▢▢▢▢▢

KING OF THE HILL: A standard King of the Hill game with no Shields.

Weapons

Falcon 2
Mauler
Cyclone
Laptop Gun
Reaper

Simulants

TechSim:1— ▢ Perfect
TechSim:2— ▢ Hard, ▢ Perfect
CISim:1— ▢ Hard, ▢ Perfect
CISim:2— ▢ Easy, ▢ Perfect
CISim:3— ▢ Perfect

ARENA: Ruins

LIMITS: 10 minutes or Team Score: 1P—10, 2P—20, 3P—25, 4P—30

The good news is that the Simulants can't use Shields. The bad news is that the Simulants are really good. Learn the map well to give yourself an edge. Then hold onto those hills. A tie will result in a win for you, so make a point or make sure that they can't make any.

 Unlocking Challenge 26 also unlocks the Ruins Arena in multiplayer.

Ruins

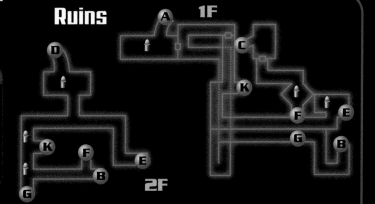

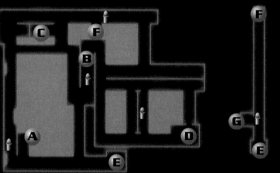

Sewers

Mid Levels **Top Levels**

challenge 27 ☐☐☐☐☐

HACKER CENTRAL: A Hacker Central game featuring Rocket
Launchers and expert opponents.

Weapons
Falcon 2
MagSec 4
CMP150
Rocket Launcher
Shield

Simulants
CIASim:1— ▢ Perfect
FBISim:1— ▢ Perfect
CIASim:2— ▢ Perfect
FBISim:2— ▢ Perfect

ARENA: Sewers

LIMITS: 10 minutes or Team Score 10

Every Simulant is set at Perfect Difficulty. That means trouble
for you. But a tie is as good as a win, so a stalemate can be a
good thing. The Rocket Launcher is deadly and hazardous in
the tight hallways of the Sewers. The best use is to blast an
opponent who is downloading or as a suicide run against
someone holding the Data Uplink.

Sub Levels

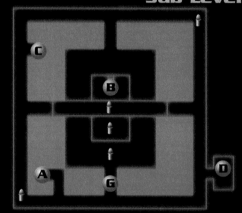

challenge 28 ☐☐☐☐☐

CAPTURE THE CASE: A Capture the Case game with no Shields, but
expert opponents.

Weapons
Falcon 2
Falcon 2 (silencer)
DY357 Magnum
AR34
Shotgun

Simulants
GuardSim:1— ▢ Dark
GuardSim:2— ▢ Dark
GuardSim:3— ▢ Dark
GuardSim:4— ▢ Dark
GuardSim:5— ▢ Dark

ARENA: Villa

LIMITS: 10 minutes or Team Score 9

When playing a one-player game you can try the keep-away
method and hope for a tie. Grab the opponent's case and wait
them out. But there are only two of them, right? An assault
on the enemy who has your case can lead to a score. Study
the map and know where your enemies will come from.

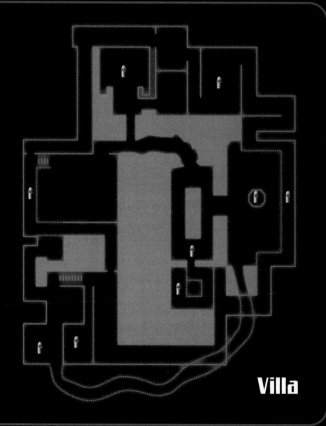

Villa

**Opening Challenge 28 will also unlock DarkSim—the
baddest Simulant on the block—for multiplayer games.**

CHALLENGES

PERFECT DARK™

challenge 29 ☐☐☐☐☐☐

COMBAT: Standard combat with no Shields available. Weapons include the DY357 and the Dragon.

Weapons

- Falcon 2
- Cyclone
- DY357 Magnum
- CMP150
- Dragon

Simulants

WorkSim:1—	Dark
WorkSim:2—	Dark
GuardSim:1—	Dark
GuardSim:2—	Dark
GuardSim:3—	Dark

ARENA: G5 Building

LIMITS: 10 minutes or Team Score: 1P—10, 2P—20, 3P—25, 4P—30

No tricks can get you through this easily. It's a slugfest from start to finish. The Simulants are ruthless and efficient. Find fast-firing weapons and put your back to a wall. Do not, however, stop moving. By now you should be an accomplished agent, but this is a tough one.

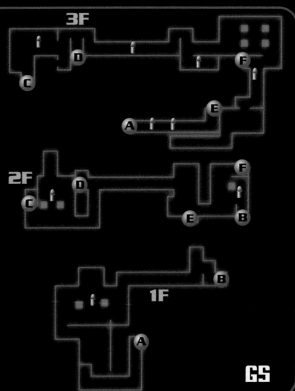

challenge 30 ☐☐☐☐☐☐

KING OF THE HILL: A pistols-only King of the Hill game against elite opposition.

Weapons

- Falcon 2
- Falcon 2 (scope)
- MagSec 4
- Mauler
- DY357 Magnum

Simulants

BlondSim:1—	Dark
CassSim—	Dark
JoSim:1—	Normal (on your team)
TrentSim—	Dark
BlondeSim:2—	Dark
BlondeSim:3—	Dark

ARENA: Skedar

LIMITS: 10 minutes or Team Score: 1P—10, 2P—20, 3P—25, 4P—30

You get a Simulant on your team to help even things up a bit, but she's only at Normal Difficulty, so mainly she just draws enemy fire. Still, against these opponents you need all the help you can get. You should use standard King of the Hill tactics, but be prepared for the extremely fast and accurate onslaughts the Simulants throw at you. They won't give you any breathing room.

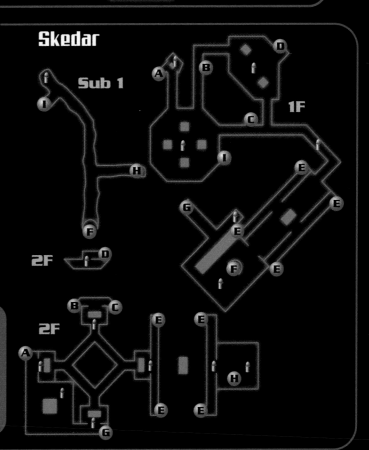

MISSION 01

SIGNAL : STABLE

dataDyne Central–Defection

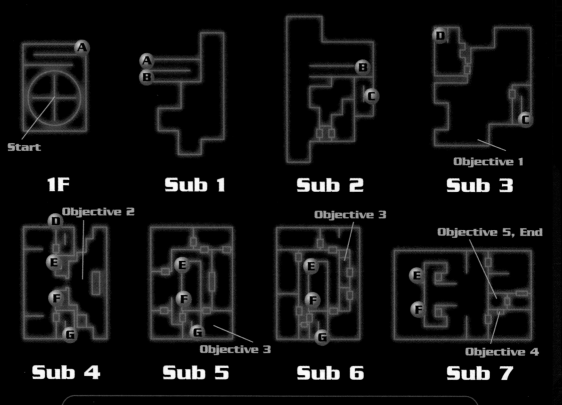

A — Start

1F

A
B

Sub 1

B
C

Sub 2

D
C — Objective 1

Sub 3

Objective 2
D
E
F
G

Sub 4

E
F
G — Objective 3

Sub 5

Objective 3
E
F
G

Sub 6

Objective 5, End
E
F
Objective 4

Sub 7

The circled letters (A) show where the different floors connect. They indicate stairs, ramps, elevators, even holes in the ground.

Background

A dataDyne scientist calling himself Dr. Caroll has contacted the Carrington Institute requesting that we rescue him from the dataDyne headquarters tonight. He claims that he has complained to dataDyne about the moral implications of his current project, but rather than dismiss him, they will mentally restructure him until he finds the nature of the project acceptable again.

Carrington//This is your first mission, Joanna, and it could hardly be more vital to us. We need to get Dr. Caroll out of there before anything happens to him, and we also need to know about dataDyne's future plans. Our standard rules of engagement apply; do not kill unarmed civilians. Remember, the code keys only work if their owners are alive.

PERFECT DARK

6 5 6 5 6 5 6 8 6 5 4 1 2 1 0 2 0 0 1 2 2 1 0 0 0 0 0 1
4 1 4 5 4 6 5 4 1 5 0 5 6 5 0 4 1 7 6 6 5 4 1 1 5

OBJECTIVES

★ ★ 1. Disable internal security hub

★ ★ 2. Obtain keycode necklace.

★ 3. Download project files

★ ★ 4. Disable external comms hub

★ ★ ★ 5. Gain entrance to laboratory

Look for the numbers in the red-bordered screenshots in the walkthrough.
They indicate which objective is being accomplished.

★ AGENT ★ SPECIAL AGENT ★ PERFECT AGENT

Your first objective is to disable the internal security hub. From the start point on the helipad, creep to the edge in front of you and to the left. Shoot out both the security camera and the guard below.

Drop straight down from your perch and pass through the two grated doors. A guard awaits you around the first corner. There are two security cameras in this room. You can see this first one from here.

NOTE
Stick to your trusty silenced Falcon 2 for now. It's more accurate and makes better use of ammo than the CMP150s you'll pick up from the guards. Save the CMP150 and its precious ammo for later.

Lean against the railing before the ramp leading down and look above the ramp. There's the second camera. A couple of shots to each should give you some privacy.

1 Head down the ramp and look for the bright red panel nearby. Pull out your ECM Mines and plant one on the screen.

Now it's time to find Cassandra's necklace. Go through the grated door at the other end of the room and head down the stairwell. Dispatch any guards on the way down as well as the ones beyond the door at the bottom.

2 Run past the elevators and look at one of the tables on the right. Push this button.

2 Go through the double doors between the elevators. Put away your weapons and make your entrance. Cassandra immediately gives you attitude, which makes it easier to do what you're about to do. Smack her and rob her of her keycode necklace. *Be sure not to kill her.* The keycode only works if she's alive.

Time to do some downloading. As you exit Cassandra's office, go left and through the brown door next to the elevator. Use these stairs to get down to the next floor. Open the door at the bottom of the stairs and fire away at the guards behind it

After you clear them out, walk past the two elevators and slowly peek around the corner to your right. Smile for the camera before you put a bullet through the lens. If you take another route, you can destroy the camera from behind by going through

From here, visit every room on this floor and take care of all the guards. You'll be glad you did later. Be sure to keep an eye out for ammo boxes sitting on tables.

Return to the stairwell and continue down to the last floor. More guards await you on this floor. Eliminate as many as you can from the stairwell using the door for cover.

Directly to your left is a locked door you can't open without help. Don't worry about it for now. Work your way down the hall, cleaning out the two rooms across from the elevators. There is one guard in each room.

Around the next corner, you'll fi a set of double doors with a guard behind it. Shoot him and run through the door to the left Another guard awaits.

NONE
If you've been noisy on this floor, you may have already encountered the Shock Trooper after you eliminated the guards beyond the double door.

Exit back through the double doors and down the long hall. You need to disable a security camera beyond the door. Peek your head through the doors just enough to shoot it out.

With the camera gone, continue through the door and around the corner until you see two doors on your left. Behind the first one is a guard who'll drop Double Falcons. Grab it and start double-fisting.

3 When you try to open the second door, you overhear a programmer talking about deleting files. When the man comes out of door, he yells for security. Too bad him; you've disposed of them all.

NONE
If you get too close to the programmer, he'll give up and won't lead you to the Laptop Gun. If this happens, back off until he runs off, screaming for security. Then follow him.

3 Keep a distance from him as he runs and he'll lead you to that locked door by the elevator. Grab the extra ammo and the Laptop Gun—you'll need it later.

3 Once you've looted the room, follow him to the left elevator and call it for him. He takes you up one floor and leads you to a room with two terminals.

3 As you enter the room, immediately switch to your Data Uplink. As soon as he says, "Rig I'm in…," start your download. (can kill him if you choose.) If you don't do this in time, you'll fail y mission, so stay on your toes.

MIPS
While still crouching, creep to the edge of the stairs to safely take out any stragglers.

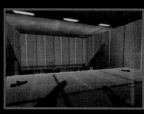

Now, back to the elevators. Take the left one all the way down to the lobby and be prepared for a gunfight. Keep an eye out for a bunch of Shock Troopers

Crouch all the way down as you leave the elevator and turn around to face the guards. From this vantage point, you can easily pick off the first few as they come

4 Stand back up and head down the stairs. The door to your right holds your fourth objective and several Shock Troopers. Dispose of them as safely as you can, using the door and walls for cover.

4 Here it is. Throw another ECM Mine on this panel and exit.

Go past the stairs and stop at the next door. There is a small army behind this door, so pull out your Laptop Gun; you'll enjoy this.

The Laptop Gun also functions as a Sentry Gun, which you can deploy by firing with the Reload button held down. Aim squarely in front of the door and deploy the Sentry Gun.

Open the door to let them know you're here. Now back off and let the carnage ensue. Wait around the corner so that you can safely dispatch any guards who may slip by the Sentry Gun.

5 When the gunfire subsides, run through the door and to the right, watching for any Troopers that may have survived. A wall opens to reveal an elevator behind it. Jump on—you're finished.

Co-Operative Notes

After obtaining Cassandra's keycode, one player can head two floors down and start dealing with the programmer. In the meantime, the second player can head one floor down and start clearing it of guards. Don't forget the camera. Meet up in the computer room where you'll download the files.

dataDyne Research-Investigation

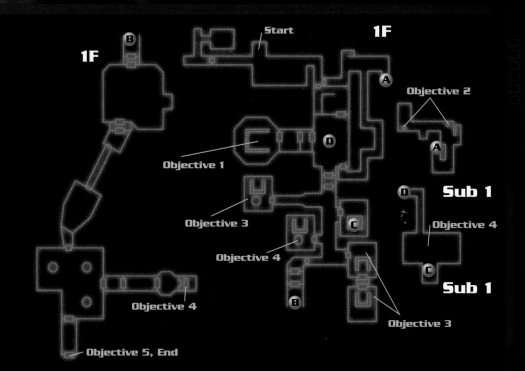

Start
1F
1F
B
A
Objective 2
A
D
Objective 1
D
Sub 1
Objective 3
C
Objective 4
Objective 4
C
B
Sub 1
Objective 4
Objective 3
Objective 5, End

Carrington//You'll need to use your remote comlink to get past the door to the sector where Dr. Caroll's lab is located. Unfortunately, we've detected huge levels of electro-magnetic activity around the laboratories which interfere with all our communications equipment. Convince the scientists to shut their experiments down. Remember that they are noncombatants, so don't kill them. And don't forget your Data Uplink; it may come in handy.

MISSION 01

OBJECTIVES

★ ★ ★ 1. Holograph radioactive isotope

★ ★ 2. Start security maintenance cycle

★ ★ 3. Shut down experiments

★ 4. Obtain experimental technologies

★ ★ ★ 5. Locate Dr. Caroll

Look for the numbers in the red-bordered screenshots in the walkthrough.
They indicate which objective is being accomplished.

★ AGENT   ★ SPECIAL AGENT   ★ PERFECT AGENT

As the elevator doors open, head to your left and take down the guard that is on patrol. Round the corner and go through the silver door. Clear this room of guards.

2 Once the lobby is empty, return through the silver door. Look to your right at the maintenance door made of vertical panels. Wait here for a maintenance bot to open it and proceed through.

2 Walk down this narrow corridor into a large room. Pass the hallway on your right and turn down the hallway at the end of the room. Open the door and shoot the two guards in here.

To safely shoot these two guards, stand against the door and aim through the window. If your timing is right, you can get off two headshots without ever being seen.

2 With the room clear, go straight down the hallway, ignoring the room on the right, until you reach a computer on the wall. Turn the corner to see a second terminal.

2 Activate the second terminal on the left wall first to reprogram the bots. Then, activate the first terminal you came across to activate the bots. Objective 2 complete!

NOTE
In the room you passed on the right, there is a terminal that will release a security locker (if you have gone unseen until now). See the Secrets section for more details.

Now head back through the door and turn down the sloped left hallway you passed earlier. Follow this hallway through five guards until you reach a silver door.

This large room should be clear of enemies if you cleaned out the lobby area earlier. Turn to your left and enter the large silver door with "Caution" written on it.

1 Behind the next door are two guards. Take them down and bring out your CamSpy. Use your CamSpy to enter the third silver door by pressing Ⓑ.

1 So that's what an isotope looks like? Navigate your CamSpy through the radioactive room until you have a close-up of the radioactive isotope. Snap a picture by pressing your trigger. Now that Objective 1 is complete, take the CamSpy to Joanna's feet to return it.

Exit the room and enter the door to your right that reads "Sector Two." Shoot the guard there and open the next door. From this spot you can take down a lot of guards safely. Use the door as a shield when you need to reload.

3 Once you have a clear hallway, take the first right and open the door. Behind this door is a set of guards and the first of three experiments you have to shut down.

6665566565865 210 00121 21000001
5866566 700 0 5

3 Find the scientist and stick your pistol to his head. He will be happy to assist you in shutting down the experiment. Don't forget to collect the two boxes of ammo from this room before leaving.

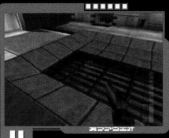

4 Now return to the main hallway and enter the next room you come across on your left side. In this room is a grating on the floor and a hydraulic platform. Stand next to the grating and aim through it at the soldier standing next to a scientist.

4 You're about to ruin his day. Be sure to take him down with one headshot to avoid return fire. Once he is on his back, take the platform down and collect his gun. Hmmm… an experimental weapon.

TIPS Don't go wild with your new K7 Avenger just yet. This experimental weapon will come in handy later, so save your ammo.

4 Now that you have acquired experimental item 1, you can collect the ammo back near the grating and continue on your way. Continue down the main hallway and dispose of any guards, then visit the next room on the right.

4 A glass case surrounds experimental item 2. Shoot or punch out the glass and grab the Night Vision glasses. Two down, one to go! There are two boxes of ammo in this room as well.

3 Now make your way to the main hall and enter the last room on the left. There may be two guards left in this hallway. Go through the door and take out the two guards waiting for you. Grab the ammo and find the scientist. Exchange a few words with him and he'll cooperate in shutting down his experiment.

3 On one wall of this room is a large metal door. Open this door and the next one. When you enter, you find another scientist. This one is not as helpful as the others are. When he is told to shut down his experiments, he walks over to a terminal and activates the alarm.

3 To avoid his friends with guns, follow him to the terminal. When he stops at a screen, give him a knuckle sandwich. The terminal he was standing at is the alarm. Use Ⓑ to activate the remaining terminals to shut down his experiment.

WARNING! *Do not kill the scientists or you will fail your mission.* If you feel the need to punish them for their wrongdoing, you can simply punch them.

Now that all three experiments are shut down, Objective 3 is complete. Now return to the main hall and enter the last remaining door. There are two guards behind this door and two more run to their aid. Dispose of them and enter the "Sector Three" door.

You are now standing in front of a hallway of laser locks. You didn't kill those little maintenance bots, did you? Wait for the bot to drop the lasers, and pass through as it does. It opens the door at the end of the hall, so be prepared to shoot the guard it exposes.

Behind the next door is another lobby area guarded by two soldiers. Bust a cap in them and collect the ammo on both sides of the table. Run through the next set of doors.

MISSION 1

WALKTHROUGH

Two dataDyne Shock Troopers are just inside the room with the small terminal. They have Dragons to shoot you with, so be careful. You can shoot the left guard from the hallway. The right guard then comes through the door. Blast him!

Use your Data Uplink on the terminal to gain access to the next door. When you establish a connection, two guards rush from the door behind you. Throw a Dragon against the outer door as a Proximity Mine to eliminate them.

Once you've dealt with them, restart your connection and acquire the password. Then enter the next series of doors until you reach the large "Sector Four" door.

Look out! The three Shock Troopers in this room have heavy artillery. Take them down as best you can and enter the door to your left marked "Security."

TIPS

Use the large "Sector Four" door as a shield when dealing with the three Shock Troopers. Try to draw them to the door to take them straight on.

4 Take these doors past three Shock Troopers and enter the small room containing a Shield Tech. Objective 4 complete!

Go back to the main room and go to the "Restricted" door to the left. Inside this room are Sentry Guns on arches over the path.

These guns fire only if you activate them by getting too close. Open the door and back away immediately. Use the scope on the K7 Avenger to do away with them.

PERFECT DARK

5 Be aware that another gun is on the backside of the first arch. You can shoot it from under the arch by using the scope and maintaining steady footing. Once you have blasted the final Sentry, you can enter the last door.

5 Objective 5 complete! You've located Dr. Caroll, but can you escort him out?

Co-Operative Notes

If you feel confident in your skills, split up early. One player can follow the maintenance bot and reprogram it. The other player can cut straight through to the isotope.

Meet up again at the door that leads to the main hallway. Watch each other's backs as you clear the hallway of pesky guards. With the guards cleared, you can split the hall down the middle. One player can take the two doors on the left, the other the first two doors on the right. Team up for the last door on the right.

Don't forget to have one player guard the door behind the terminals while the other is cracking the password.

dataDyne Central-Extraction

Objective 5

8F

7F

6F

Objective 4

5F

Objective 3

Objective 2

Objective 1   Start

4F

3F

2F

1F

MISSION 01

Background

The alarm has been given, and there are dataDyne Shock Troops ready for you throughout the building. Exit via the foyer is impossible due to the number of ground troops present. The transport will collect you and Dr. Caroll from the helipad.

Carrington//I don't have to remind you to protect Dr. Caroll at all costs, Joanna. Cassandra and dataDyne are going to be throwing all the obstacles they can in your path to prevent you from getting Dr. Caroll out. Good Luck.

OBJECTIVES

★ ★ ★ 1. Access foyer elevator

★ ★ 2. Reactivate office elevator

★ ★ 3. Destroy dataDyne Hovercopter

★ ★ ★ 4. Defeat Cassandra's bodyguards

★ ★ ★ 5. Rendezvous at helipad

Look for the numbers in the red-bordered screenshots in the walkthrough.
They indicate which objective is being accomplished.

★ AGENT   ★ SPECIAL AGENT   ★ PERFECT AGENT

walkthrough

NONE

Whatever you do, don't shoot the floating thing in front of you. That's Dr. Caroll! He's the one you've got to protect.

The lights are out, but they won't stay out long. Luckily, you just pilfered the experimental Night Vision. Strap it on and take a step forward to open the door and reveal a guard. He can't see you from there if you're quiet, so pop him in the head.

Grab the guard's CMP150 and turn left to face a sliding door. Stay as far left as you can. Open the door and immediately take a few steps back. The idea is to gain some distance between you and the guard, but also to be standing still when he finally comes into view.

As you pass through the door, you'll notice an opening to your left. Now, slowly strafe to your right, staying close to the wall and keeping the opening in view. Pick off each of the two guards as they become visible.

Go through the opening and stop. You can just make out the heads of two guards peeking out from above and to the right. Take careful aim and fire.

Turn to your right and you'll see another Shock Trooper's head peeking out from behind a barricade down the hall. Again, this guy won't see you. Have your way with him.

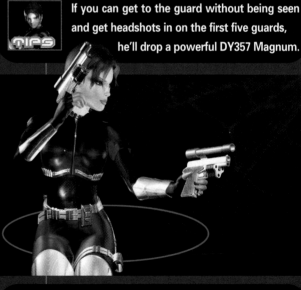

TIPS

If you can get to the guard without being seen and get headshots in on the first five guards, he'll drop a powerful DY357 Magnum.

TIPS

Ammo is scarce on this level. Don't leave any bodies unsearched.

Continue down this hallway and carefully peek to your left. There are two anxious guards waiting behind the desk. If you've been quick, the lights will still be out and they won't see you. Punish them for their incompetence.

Past the desk and to the left awaits the final guard before you reach the elevators. Nail him and move on.

8665566565866649210012000122100000018

1 Following the hallway, you reach the stairs leading to the elevators. Only one of them works, so hop on and you'll have the first objective in the bag.

At the top, go past the elevators until you see a set of double doors. Take a right and surprise the guard waiting there.

4 Go through the door behind his corpse and follow the corridor until you see two doors on the left. As you approach the second door, two of Cassandra's bodyguards pop out at you with shotguns. Waste 'em.

Watch out for the chopper outside the windows too. You'll deal with it later. For now, stay out of its way.

The chopper circles the building, so if you get caught in its gunfire just retreat into a room until it moves on.

4 Take a left where the two bodyguards appeared and walk to the next room. Through the door straight ahead you'll find another bodyguard and a computer terminal.

It's a good idea to start using the Shotguns that the bodyguards drop. You'll need the more accurate sights of your other weapons a little later.

2 Terminate the bodyguard and activate the terminal to unlock the office elevator. Another objective is complete.

Backtrack quickly to the elevators and take the first one up to the next floor. Make your way around the second corner and face two Shock Troopers.

Your goal is the double doors next to the barricades. Turn left and pass through the sliding wall behind the chair.

4 Continue through one more door and find more bodyguards. Show them what you think of them and press on.

4 Through the next door, the other elevator should be visible. Walk straight ahead and into the last room to check for any more bodyguards. That done, head out and through the door next to the elevator.

Climb the stairs to the next floor and turn right. You'll catch a dataDyne Shock Trooper and a couple of scientists standing around a weapon.

Blast the Trooper and watch the scientists run. What's this? A Rocket Launcher! Hmmm.... What can you use this thing on?

3 Equip the Launcher and step to the window. You only have one shot, so make it count.

MISSION 01

walkthrough

Once you acquire the Rocket Launcher, lure the chopper to the corner room near the stairs you came up on. Then back up so you're standing by the door. The chopper will have problems shooting around the post and you'll have a free shot at it.

NOTE

If you miss with the Rocket Launcher, you can still down the chopper with your other weapons. This takes a lot of ammo, however, and may leave you strapped when you face Cassandra later on.

Through the door next to where you picked up the Rocket Launcher is a set of stairs. Take these up to the very top where a grated door awaits.

As you go through the door, you'll find Cassandra and five bodyguards waiting for you. You've got a few seconds to find a good defense spot while she's yapping away.

Across from the grated door is the ramp leading up to the catwalk. Crouch as low as you can and hide behind it while facing the ramp.

4 The lights go out and you're left to tangle with these guards. Use your Night Vision. This is where your more accurate guns come in handy. Peek to the right until you can see the guard by the fan.

4 Your next target is the guard on the second level. While staying close to the left wall, back up a bit until you can see the guard's head. Pop a cap in it.

4 Now slowly scoot to your right, while still crouching, until you can see another guard. Carefully dispose of her.

4 You can rid yourself of her two remaining friends the same way.

Once you've blasted all of Cassandra's bodyguards, head up the ramp and out the door. Take off your Night Vision and make your way up to the helipad.

5 Joanna makes it out alive—mission accomplished!

Co-Operative Notes

This quick and dirty level requires some tight teamwork. You'll face heavy gunfire in this one, so stick together and watch each other's backs.

Decide before you reach the top floor which of Cassandra's bodyguards you'll be aiming for. You don't want to waste ammo shooting at the same object as your teammate is. Shoot different ones and you'll eliminate more guards quickly.

MISSION 02

Carrington Villa-Hostage One

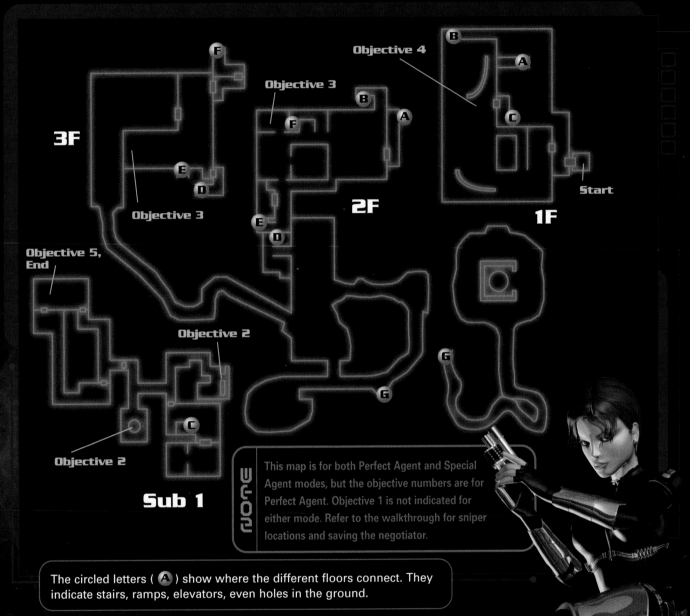

3F

2F

1F

Sub 1

Objective 4

Objective 3

Objective 3

Objective 5, End

Objective 2

Objective 2

Start

NOTE This map is for both Perfect Agent and Special Agent modes, but the objective numbers are for Perfect Agent. Objective 1 is not indicated for either mode. Refer to the walkthrough for sniper locations and saving the negotiator.

The circled letters (Ⓐ) show where the different floors connect. They indicate stairs, ramps, elevators, even holes in the ground.

Background

Daniel Carrington is being held hostage at his private villa. A message from Cassandra De Vries has laid out the terms: Daniel's life for the return of the AI known as Dr. Caroll. What dataDyne doesn't know is that the AI was at the villa when they struck. Our guess is that Daniel concealed it safely before they found him.

Carrington// Not available

NOTE: The first half of this mission requires a separate path for the Perfect Agent mode. When playing on Special Agent or Agent, follow the Special Agent walkthough.

Perfect Agent

OBJECTIVES

★★ 1. Eliminate rooftop snipers

★★★ 2. Activate wind generator

★★ 3. Locate and eliminate dataDyne hackers

★★ 4. Capture dataDyne guard

★★★ 5. Rescue Carrington

Look for the numbers in the red-bordered screenshots in the walkthrough. They indicate which objective is being accomplished.

★ AGENT ★ SPECIAL AGENT ★ PERFECT AGENT

How does she get into these situations? Joanna is held at gunpoint by two guards. Thank goodness for that Laptop Gun you are carrying. Quickly bring it out and make short work of these thugs.

1 A sniper is on the roof to the right of your captors. If you act fast, you can shoot him from where you are standing before he can fire back.

1 Now look behind you to find another sniper standing on a wall. Use the slight scope of your Laptop Gun to pluck him off.

1 Time to venture off of this pier. Grab a CMP150 as you take the plank up and go to your right. Creep slowly to the end of the deck until your see the head of a sniper poking over the roof. Give him a headshot.

Special Agent

OBJECTIVES

★★ 1. Save the negotiator

★★ 2. Eliminate rooftop snipers

★★★ 3. Activate wind generator

★★★ 4. Rescue Carrington

Look for the numbers in the red-bordered screenshots in the walkthrough. They indicate which objective is being accomplished.

★ AGENT ★ SPECIAL AGENT ★ PERFECT AGENT

You need to act fast for this one. Immediately after gaining control of Joanna, take her to the ledge directly in front of you and snipe the guards holding the negotiator at gunpoint.

 **WARNING!** If you wait too long to shoot the guards holding the negotiator, they will shoot her. Be as quick as possible to avoid starting over.

After saving the negotiator, turn to your right and circle around the telescope until you reach a path. Shoot the crate you pass for more ammo.

 TIPS You may shoot the crates throughout this level for more ammo.

Perfect Agent

1 Now walk about halfway up the stairs to your right. On your left you see another sniper poking over the rooftop. Use your Laptop to show him who the real sniper is.

Walk back down the stairs and take out your CMP150. Shoot the guard standing underneath the stairs. Then put your gun away and open the door to the villa.

4 There is a guard with his back to you on your left. He looks like he wants to be captured. Sneak up behind him and slap the back of his head. When he falls, you have completed Objective 4.

Circle around the wall to your right and sneak up behind another guard. You can shoot this one. Head up the stairs and mow down the guards that come running at you. You can use the stairwell as cover to reload.

 TIPS

If you missed punching the first guard, you can punch the second guard you sneak up on to complete Objective 4.

As you enter the room, some guards attack you from the first blue hallway on the right. Turn and shoot them all down. Once you have cleared the guards, go down the second blue hallway to your right.

Special Agent

A guard lies down in your path to shoot at you. Shoot him in the head, take his gun, and continue down the path to a ledge.

Step to the edge of the ledge and aim down at the two guards below. Once you've disposed of them, drop down. Continue on the path to the right.

1 When you come across an opening on your left, put your back against the right wall and peek around the left wall to find a sniper. Use your Sniper Rifle to take him down.

1 Go toward the fallen sniper and slowly make your way down the first flight of steps. From here, aim your rifle to the right and pluck off four snipers. Use the wall for cover if needed.

1 Continue down the steps and look left to find a few guards and another sniper on a rooftop. After you have taken care of him, continue toward the villa, making a right near the green fern.

1 Walk to the water's edge and use your Sniper Rifle's scope to see the sniper out on the wall. Put a bullet in his head and make your way back to the villa. Go up the steps leading to the balcony.

MISSION 02

02

Perfect Agent

Special Agent

Walkthrough

Turn left and enter the first door on your right. In here is a bathroom with a Sniper Rifle lying near the toilet. Wonder what it's doing here?

Now exit the room and go right, up another flight of stairs. There are two guards in front of you as well as two in the room to your left. Draw them to the top of the stairs for safer disposal.

1 From the landing atop the first flight of stairs you can shoot the last sniper (slightly to the left). Continue up the steps and enter the door.

Use your CMP150 to waste the guards to your right and in the room in front of you. Go down the steps and make a right down the first blue hallway you pass.

1 From the top of the stairs, make a right and open the door. This is tricky: Use the doorjamb as cover to take out the sniper to your left.

1 Now turn a little to your right to see the head of another sniper down below. One bullet to the skull should take him off his perch.

Blow away the two guards standing near the door and move down the stairs beside the kitchen.

Have your way with the two guards here and enter the second door on your left.

1 From the same balcony step into the right corner and face the door you came through. When you squint real hard, you can see the head of another sniper. Use your Sniper Rifle to drop him.

Take the stairs from the balcony down to ground level and make your way to the right. Turn right into the small alcove and travel through the set of hallways. Two guards patrol these halls.

1 From the top of the steps at the end of the set of hallways, you can shoot two more guards and a sniper. The sniper is on your right, just over the hill. When he is dead, you have completed Objective 1.

3 Continue into the courtyard and enter the door on your right. Does this room look familiar? Take a right and notice the computer terminals in the far corner of the room next to the stairs.

3 Now go down the steps and walk forward, past the blue hallways, until you reach another room with more computer terminals. Remember where these rooms are!

Take your first left down the blue hallway and down the stairs near the kitchen. You are back to the room you started in. Go into the second door on the left.

TIPS

It is important to remember where the rooms containing the terminals are located. When you need to eliminate the hackers, you have a very limited time and must be able to find these rooms in a hurry.

666556666669 210 2 0012 210000001
54431345554 456565558766541 6

None Perfect Agent and Special Agent meet up here and continue.

Once you open the door, make your way down the stairs and pop the few guards waiting for you. Then go through the double doors under the stairs.

2 Follow the path straight and make a right at the end. Shoot the three guards in here before going to the two control panels.

2 Take the metal paths to the small control panels. Press Ⓑ on each one to activate them. Now you must turn on the wind generator.

Look on the ground for the power cable. Follow it to the wind generator terminal. Carefully dispose of the three guards protecting it. Use the wall for cover.

2 After all the guards are laid flat, you can activate the control panel on the wind generator. Yes! Objective complete.

3 Immediately after activating the generator, head upstairs to the first room with the computer terminals. On the way, you'll be notified of the hackers.

 TIPS Time to play it safe. You only have one minute to stop the hackers, so you may want to practice the route before activating the wind generator.

3 Backtrack your way to the computer terminals in the room near the blue hallway. Shoot the hackers *without damaging the terminals* or you will fail your mission.

3 Now you must hurry up the stairs and get the last of the hackers in the room to your right. When all the hackers are dead, you have completed another objective. Now return to the door leading to the wind generator.

From the double doors, make your first left and take a right at the end of the hall. Follow the hallway around to the double doors and take the stairs down.

To your right is a Shock Trooper who turns and runs you into an ambush of two more Shock Troopers. Shoot him as he runs from you, then confront his friends.

 TIPS If you haven't already used it, you can throw your Laptop Gun—set to Sentry—into the two Troopers to avoid confrontation and preserve health. You can pick the Laptop Gun back up by pressing Ⓑ.

MISSION 02

Head back toward the stairs and enter the double doors just beyond them. Expect gunfire the second the doors open. Strafe to the side and return fire.

Use fancy sidestepping to blast your way through these Shock Troopers hiding behind bottles at every turn. Try to get headshots if you see any Troopers peeking through the bottles ahead of you.

Watch out for the Shock Troopers hiding behind these shelves. Sidestep and fire fast to get them before they get you.

S Make your way through the mess of Troopers and bottles to the double doors at the end of the gauntlet. The last Shock Trooper to fall leaves behind a key card that unlocks the double doors.

S Open the doors and *presto*! It's Carrington! Mission complete.

Co-Operative Notes

In Perfect Co-Operative mode, player 1 starts on the pier at gunpoint. Player 2 starts near the telescope on the mountain. Player 1 can take care of the captures and surrounding snipers. Player 2 can take down the remaining snipers with the Laptop Gun on the way to the upstairs.

Player 1 can now clear the bottom floor of guards while player 2 clears out the top floor. Both players can then meet on the middle floor to waste the remaining soldiers.

Have one player stay back and get ready to shoot the hackers as the other activates the wind generator. Once these two objectives are complete, you can storm the tunnels and rescue Carrington together.

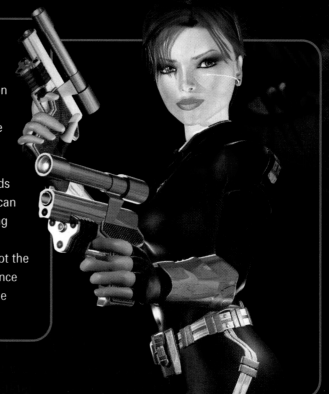

MISSION 03

Chicago-Stealth

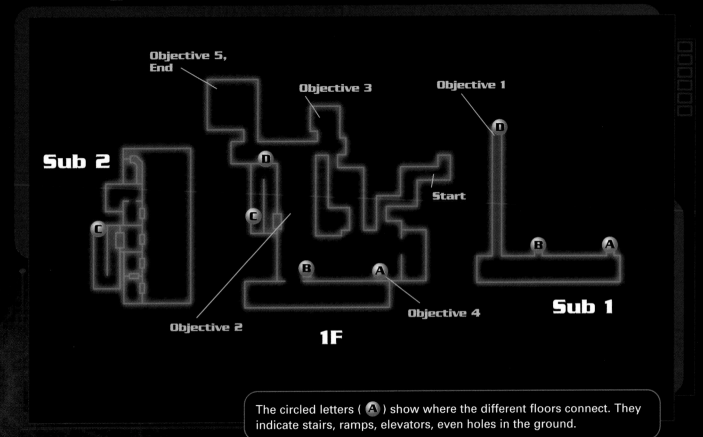

The circled letters (Ⓐ) show where the different floors connect. They indicate stairs, ramps, elevators, even holes in the ground.

Background

The G5 Corporation is believed to be a front for dataDyne. Care is needed due to civilian presence on the streets. Expect intense resistance outside and inside the building—our recon team reported that the buildup of troops started hours ago.

Carrington//Remember your urban combat training. It will come in very useful if the situation hasn't changed since the recon team's report earlier. One more thing, Joanna—there's a security robot patrolling the street. Stay away from it if at all possible.

OBJECTIVES

★ ★ ★ 1. Retrieve drop point equipment

★ 2. Attach tracer to limousine

★ ★ 3. Prepare escape route

★ ★ ★ 4. Create vehicular diversion

★ ★ ★ 5. Gain entry to G5 building

Look for the numbers in the red-bordered screenshots in the walkthrough. They indicate which objective is being accomplished.

★ AGENT ★ SPECIAL AGENT ★ PERFECT AGENT

Shhhhh! The key to this level is to be as quiet as possible to avoid bringing out more guards. Too much gunfire will make the surrounding guards call their friends, so try to isolate your enemies and take them out with quick headshots.

Civilians will blow your cover fast if they see your gun exposed. Walk down the alley and stop just short of where it turns left. Let the civilian come close to you and slap him down. If he's down, he won't get in the way.

Carefully move to your left and position yourself to get a headshot on the guard that walks out of the hallway.

In the hallway where you dropped the last soldier, there is another soldier that resembles a civilian. Stand next to the opening of the hallway and line up your sight at head level. Sidestep to put a bullet into his head.

CIA agents (wearing brown) are innocent civilians—they do not attack you and cannot be shot or your mission is a failure. FBI agents (wearing black) call for reinforcements, making Magnum-toting guards appear in droves.

Go down the hallway and turn left. Walk to the bottom of the small set of stairs opposite the taxi. Turn right and shoot the guard walking near the blue graffiti.

A robot guard that you cannot shoot down patrols back and forth through the streets. Avoid it at all costs. If it starts shooting at you too much, other guards will come to its aid. Try to time your street excursions away from it.

Another guard is on his way toward you on the sidewalk. Take a step back and quiet him as fast as possible.

Packs of guards lurk behind the rolling doors. If they hear too much gunfire, they'll open the doors and you'll face a big problem.

If all is well, no more guards patrol this part of the street. Walk along the right sidewalk until you reach the hall under the

Continue down the sidewalk and hang a right onto the next street. This street should be empty with the exception of a civilian and a

walkthrough

2 Walk to the rear of the limousine and plant your Tracer Bug on the bumper. If you take too long to complete this objective, the limousine will leave, causing you to fail. You will also fail if a CIA agent sees you.

With one of your objectives done, make a left onto the next street. Hop down the red grating to your left. Be careful not to let the fellows in the room to your right notice you dropping down.

1 Turn around and walk under the grating to find the equipment left for you. You've just completed an objective and acquired a Remote Mine and a Reprogrammer.

Now make your way back to the taxi. Follow the ditch under the building. When you are crouched under the building, snipe the guard on your right.

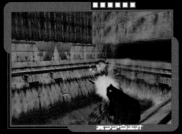

There are a few more guards around the water that you must beware of and take down quickly and quietly. There's one near the waterfall to the right, one to the left near the drain, and one on the left ledge.

4 With the sewer clear, walk up the small ramp and between the wood fences. To the right is the taxi you seek.

4 Use your Reprogrammer on the taxi. This reprograms the taxi to crash near where the limo was earlier, taking out the annoying robot guard. You can also reprogram the taxi from below if you want to be extra safe.

Now go through the hallway under the neon blue sign. Quickly punch out the two civilians in here.

Once your civilians are on the ground, push the trash bin into the stacked barrels and shoot the barrels from a distance. Step over the rubble and collect your BombSpy.

Most of the guards in the surrounding area have gone to check out the explosion. Use your BombSpy to exit this room near where the trash bin was located. Then make a left and take it past the car wreck.

Detonate the BombSpy in the center of the commotion, taking out the guards. When you have control again, step into the hallway where you used the BombSpy.

Once you are spotted, step back into the room to lure the guards after you. Shoot them as they enter the room.

Now you can jump back out and finish off the rest of them. Watch out for the civilians. A CIA agent is mixed in with them. Use ⓡ and aim at them to check their color if you get confused. Enemies will be red.

The stairs on the left have guards posted at each floor. Strafe to dodge their fire and take them down from ground level.

Mission 03

3 Climb to the top of the stairs and get out your Remote Mine. Place your Remote Mine on the concrete door. Do not detonate it or you will fail your mission.

The Mine can also be placed on the second floor. You are preparing your escape route for the next level; where you place the Mine now affects the game in the next level. Place it on the top floor for a nice surprise later.

5 Leave the stair area and head right toward the taxi wreck. Pass the wreck and make a right into a room with an elevator. Run into it and you're done.

Co-Operative Notes

This mission can be tricky using two people, because of the necessity for silence. Send one player to place the Tracer Bug on the limousine, while the other player grabs the equipment and starts the Reprogrammer on the taxi. You can meet up in the room with the BombSpy and finish out the mission.

G5 Building–Reconnaissance

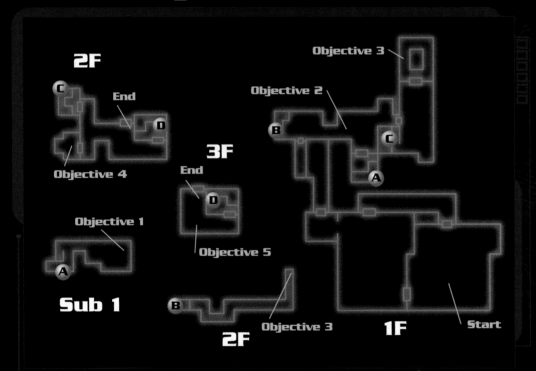

Background

Once inside G5 Headquarters, proceed into the heart of the building where the meeting should be taking place. Obtain a visual record of the meeting and get out as quickly as possible.

Carrington//The G5 Building has an integrated alarm system. Watch out for any guards who see you, as they're sure to try and activate it. This will alert the conspirators, who will almost certainly not go ahead with the meeting under such circumstances. Softly, softly, Joanna.

OBJECTIVES

★ 1. Disable damping field generator

★ ★ 2. Deactivate laser grid systems

★ ★ ★ 3. Holograph meeting conspirators

★ ★ ★ 4. Retrieve Dr. Caroll backup from safe

★ ★ ★ 5. Exit building

Look for the numbers in the red-bordered screenshots in the walkthrough.
They indicate which objective is being accomplished.

★ AGENT ★ SPECIAL AGENT ★ PERFECT AGENT

Keep your eyes peeled; the guards here make heavy use of cloaking. As soon as you start, straighten out so you're squarely facing the wall in front of you. As you do this, strafe to the far right of the room, keeping the cloaked guard in front of you.

He'll stop near the trash bin, still cloaked. Shoot him down and wait a few seconds until you see another cloaked guard move in front of you. Shoot him before he uncloaks.

When fighting cloaked guards, you can see a really faint image of them as they're moving around. Try to shoot them before they begin to uncloak. Your auto-aim doesn't work while they are fully cloaked, so make sure you manually aim at them.

Pick up the guard's key card and exit through the door. As you turn the corner, you find another guard.

The panel here controls the lights in the next room. The lights are on now, but will be triggered off when you pass a certain point in the next room. Switch them off now so that when you trigger the switch later, they'll be turned on instead of off.

...w enter the next room and find ...other door to your right. See ...se glass walls? As you pass ...m, the lights should switch on.

Passing this point not only turns on the lights, it also calls a few cloaked guards into the mix. Back through this point and keep an eye on the room.

Stay in this little part of the room for some cover as you pick off the guards. Notice the space on the left of the door where you can hide and reload as you're fighting.

The key to fighting these guys is to shoot them in their grainy, cloaked stage. Then, whether they're down or not, take cover and reload while they're firing at you. When they stop firing, pop out and retaliate.

WALKTHROUGH

The last guy down drops another key card for you. Before you use it to go through the next door, shoot through the glass at the guard behind it.

In the next little hallway, you find stairs to another door. Be careful. When you open the door, there are three guards to contend with.

Wait until the guard walks by toward your right and bust through. Quickly disable him from the back and run until you see a door on your right.

Just past the door is an alarm panel on the wall. This is what you must protect. Put your back to it and you should see another guard coming at you.

NOTE No matter how sloppy you get with cleaning up the three guards in this room, don't let them touch this panel. If they hit it, the conspirators will be alerted and your mission will fail.

If you haven't seen the third guard yet, return to the door through which you came. Walk past it and look around the corner to your left. Voilà!

2 If you've done this right, no other guards should have been alerted. Look for the four green panels on the wall. Shut them all off and you not only accomplish one objective, but you open up the path to holograph the conspirators.

Look through the glass of the door next to the alarm. You see some stairs leading down. Open the door and back up quickly to avoid the guard on the stairs. Now slowly walk toward the open doorway until you can see his head. Put a hole through it.

At the bottom of the steps, turn right and duck down. Creep along the right wall until you near its end. As more of the room opens up on your right, you see two guards chillin' under the ramp.

Look straight ahead again. Behind the last post in front of you is another guard. Carefully put him out of his misery.

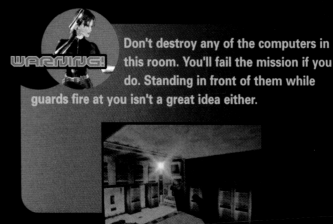

WARNING! Don't destroy any of the computers in this room. You'll fail the mission if you do. Standing in front of them while guards fire at you isn't a great idea either.

1 With the goons all gone, activate the scrolling screen to disable the damping field generator. With this objective out of the way, return to the room with the alarm.

PERFECT DARK

Behind the locked door on your right is a guard with his back to you. Shoot him in the head and return to the other end of the room, where the stairs are.

Climb the stairs and follow the catwalk to its end. Crouch down and follow the wires on the ground until you can see the door where you last shot the guard through the glass.

Stop just above it and deploy your CamSpy. You're going to have to be quick. When your CamSpy follows the wires into the next room, it has a chance of being spotted by guards.

3 Speed it through into the next room, still following the wires, until you find the conspirators.

Yet another objective completed. Man, you're good! Now crawl forward until you drop down. Be ready to take out any guards that may be patrolling.

NOTE

There is an alarm here. Try to keep the guards from activating it, but it won't ruin your mission if they do. Because you've already holographed the conspirators, all it means is more guards. If they do activate it, be sure to turn it off.

Just to the left of the alarm is a door that leads to a stairwell. Watch for guards patrolling here and go to the top.

Open the door and look right to find two guards down the hall.

Walk toward their corpses and look left as the wall ends. More guards!

The first two guards you took out on this floor were guarding the safe room. Go in and notice a large blue door in the back and a

Pull out your Door Decoder and throw it on the panel. It takes one minute for it to access the door and open it for you.

Unfortunately, the Decoder sets off the alarm. This means you're going to have to fend off an army of guards that try to enter this

:STABLE

If you stand to the right of the door, you can create a narrow line of sight through the door. The enemies almost line up in front of you. Easy pickings.

Keep an eye on the ammo in your clip. If you're running low on ammo, or if there's a lull in the swarm of enemies, close the door. Use this cover to reload and then reopen the door once you have a fresh clip.

4 When your minute is up, grab the backup disk from the safe.

5 Remember Chicago and which floor you put the Mine on in the last level? Now's the time to detonate it. After the explosion, run out the door. Make a left and then a right into a small hallway.

If you placed the Mine on the second floor in Chicago, you'll find your exit here, to the left. This is also true if you are playing in Agent mode.

5 Follow the hallway until you find another set of stairs. Climb that to the top and you're home free.

If you placed the Mine on the top floor in Chicago, you'll find an N-Bomb here.

Co-Operative Notes

A second set of eyes is very useful on this level, especially with the cloaked guards. Between you and your partner, you should be able to keep the whole room in view at all times to prevent an ambush.

A good time to split tasks is after deactivating the laser grid systems. Send one player downstairs to deal with the dampening field. Use the other player to send the CamSpy through to holograph the conspirators.

While the safe is decoding, post your players on either side of the door and pick off the opponents as they stumble in.

MISSION 04

Area 51-Infiltration

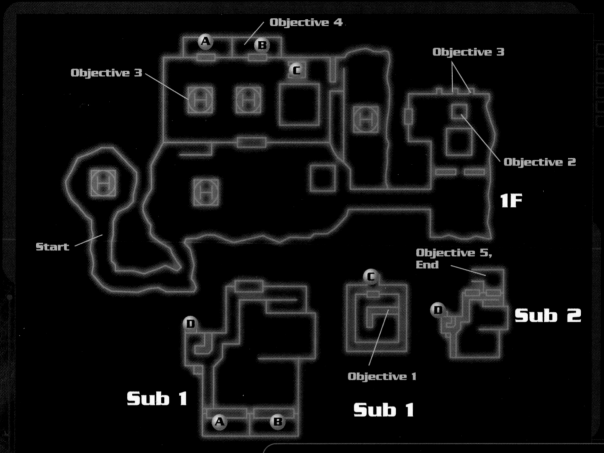

The circled letters (Ⓐ) show where the different floors connect. They indicate stairs, ramps, elevators, even holes in the ground.

Background

A craft carrying Institute advisors has been shot down in Nevada. Debris from the crash and the bodies of the advisors have been taken to Area 51. A spy inside the base has managed to get footage to the Institute of a possible survivor. This mission is to rescue that survivor.

Carrington//This is a disaster for us, Joanna. We need to get our ally out of there before it becomes too late. And there was some special equipment inside the craft, as well, which must not remain in Trent Easton's clutches. You'll have some support on this mission in the form of our spy inside Area 51 who is disguised as a guard.

OBJECTIVES

★ ★ ★ 1. Shut down air intercept radar

 ★ ★ 2. Plant comms device on antenna

  ★ 3. Disable all Robot Interceptors

★ ★ ★ 4. Gain access to hangar lift

★ ★ ★ 5. Make contact with CI spy

Look for the numbers in the red-bordered screenshots in the walkthrough.
They indicate which objective is being accomplished.

★ AGENT ★ SPECIAL AGENT ★ PERFECT AGENT

2 1 0 1 1 2   2   6 6 6 6 6 6 6 6 6 6 6 6

WALKTHROUGH

Whoa! You need to find cover, and fast. As you start this level, back up and strafe to the left until you're behind this pillar against the mountain.

Instead of peeking out to pick off your assailants, wait. They'll come around and you can get them one by one.

Don't forget to watch your back here. With the pillar to your left, a few guards may ambush you on your right.

Pick up the MagSec 4s and any Grenades they may have dropped. Don't bother with the turret gun beyond the helipad. Instead, walk the other way and around the corner.

A little farther down, you'll see another turret gun. There's no way around this one, so use the scope on your MagSec to blast it from a distance.

Throwing a Grenade at the turret gun is much easier than using a pistol. Save at least two Grenades for later though; you'll need them.

Continue down this chasm until you see an opening. There is another turret gun on the left, so peep out just enough to hit it with your pistol.

As you enter the open area, look to your right and you'll see a guard tower with two guards. If you've got keen enough eyes, you can use your Falcon 2 to pick them off. If not, use the less accurate MagSec with its built-in scope.

Run past the tower to see a fence on the left side with a hole in it. Deal with the guards who may be running up from the tunnel to your right.

Did you save a Grenade? Pull it out and throw it through the hole in the fence. You want it to land in the snow between the helipad and the fence.

The Grenade will set off the land mines so that you can safely grab the Rocket Launcher.

Now return to the tower and climb up its ladder. At the top, press the red button to open the gate below.

3

Hurry down the ladder but don't go through the gate just yet. Beyond it are a mechanic and one of the Robot Interceptors you need to destroy. Aim your only rocket through the gate and fire.

NOTE

If you want the Phoenix in the next level, you must keep the mechanic alive. Lure him away from the Interceptor, knock him out, then blow it up.

PERFECT DARK

86556565606554 2100 7 00122 2100000 1
4444 16 1 654 65 1 58685 5 56766 5 2 6

NONE If you don't destroy this interceptor now, it'll haunt you later from the air. The only difference is that it'll be shooting at you. Don't give it a chance.

With that done, run back to the tunnel near the fence. At the end of it, you'll find more guards on either side of the tunnel and a turret gun beyond. Carefully eliminate these threats and move on.

Move out into the open area and face the antenna. Looks a little high to throw your Comms Rider on it, doesn't it? You're going to have to lower it.

Quickly run across this little bridge and to the right. There is a turret gun to your left that you are avoiding.

3 While you're safely behind the antenna, you can accomplish two of your objectives. To complete Objective 3, blow up the two Robot Interceptors you can see from here with your weapon of choice.

On the base of the antenna is a green button you can use to lower the antenna to within throwing distance. Go ahead and push, still being wary of the turret gun.

NONE You can destroy this turret gun if you like. You'll be able to run around a little more freely if you do. It's not necessary, however, so do it at your own risk.

2 Chuck your Comms Rider at the satellite dish and you'll have another mission objective in the bag.

Make your way back to the helipad behind the fence. Throw a Grenade behind it to set off the land mines there. You'll notice an opening in the left wall.

NONE If you're out of Grenades, you can enter the next room through the main gate. This is quite dangerous because of the turret guns, so it's best to sneak in the back way.

When you emerge, you'll be facing a wall. Follow it to the left until it ends. From here, you can blow up the turret guns with ease.

Turn around and walk past the hole you came out of. Make a left and edge along the wall on your left side. At the end of it, on the left, you'll see another turret gun to smash.

With the turrets gone, jump down this hole and go through the metal door.

MISSION 04

walkthrough

1 Make your way to the back of the room and place your Explosives on the computer panel there.

Quick! The place is going to blow. Watch out for the lasers. Crouch down to get through the last set. The Explosives set off the alarms. Bust through the guards as quickly as you can and climb back up the stairs.

4 Remember the first Robot Interceptor you blew up in this yard? Well, you also blew up its pilot. Look around this area for a key card. He won't be needing it.

With the key card, you can open the ridged doors that lead to two different elevators. The panels used to open them are on either side of the doors.

The elevator on the right holds a couple of guards. Both elevators lead to the same place, so unless you want a confrontation, choose the left elevator.

4 This elevator opens into a large room with lots of crates and bad guys. There are two ways to mow them down. One is to stay on the elevator and use it for cover as it goes up and down.

The other way—the gung-ho way—is to move into this area and use the crates for cover. Make sure to watch your back. A lot of guards are here, including a bunch on the catwalk above. Keep moving and watch out for Grenades.

Once the room is safely cleared of guards, make your way to the back of the room to find a ramp. Use the ramp to access the catwalk that leads to an elevator door.

Use the elevator to go down a level. When the door opens, you'll have one guard in your face and another a little way down.

This level looks exactly like the one you were just in. Follow the catwalk and go down the ramp. Watch out for the guards at the bottom.

5 Just underneath the ramp, you'll find a metal door. This is it. Run through it to meet up with the CI Spy.

Co-Operative Notes

Stay together on this one until you reach the tower for the first time. Then, have one player get the Rocket Launcher and blow up the Interceptor. The other player should venture down the tunnel a bit and start eliminating the bad guys. Don't venture past the tunnel, however. There are a lot of guards beyond, so wait for your partner to join you.

When you're shutting down the air intercept radar, have one person guard the entrance. When the alarm goes off, you'll have a doorman to greet your incoming visitors.

The hangar is one of the more dangerous areas. Work this one together and cover each other's backs.

Area 51-Rescue

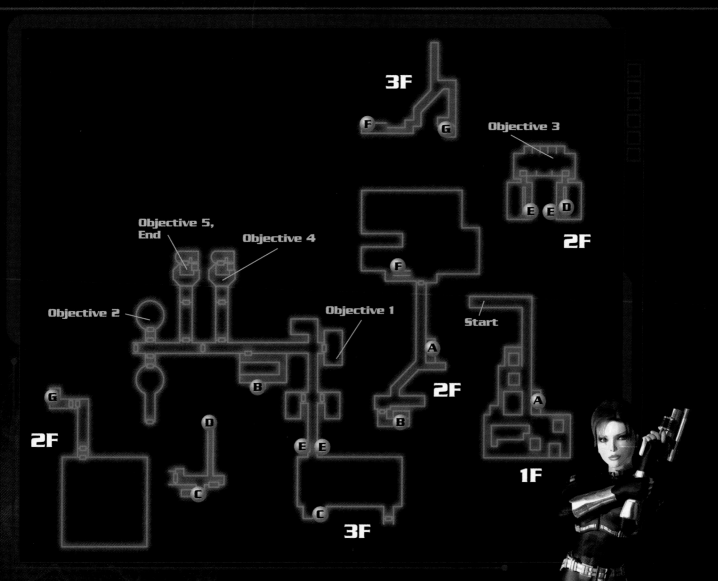

3F

F   G

Objective 3

E E D

2F

Objective 5,
End

Objective 4

Objective 2

F

Objective 1

Start

A

G

2F

B

A

2F

D

1F

B

E E

C

C

3F

Carrington//You need to cover our tracks and rescue our friend as fast as you can. A Disguise will help you do that, but it won't last forever, so make good use of it. Wipe out their records, and make sure there are no more survivors we are unaware of. Time is pressing, so hurry.

OBJECTIVES

★ 1. Destroy computer records

★★ 2. Locate conspiracy evidence

★★★ 3. Obtain and use lab technician Disguise

★★★ 4. Gain access to autopsy lab

★★★ 5. Rescue the crash survivor

Look for the numbers in the red-bordered screenshots in the walkthrough.
They indicate which objective is being accomplished.

★ AGENT   ★ SPECIAL AGENT   ★ PERFECT AGENT

Mission 04

walkthrough

You start this level behind a crate. Walk past it and take the corner to your right. The ramp here opens up into a large warehouse. Don't move into the warehouse just yet.

Try to pick off any guards you can see from the ramp. This draws many of the guards from their posts. Lure them toward the safety of your ramp and fire away.

WARNING!

The guards here may carry Grenades. It could be fatal if one catches you off guard.

When you feel you've cleared most of the guards on this floor, venture into the warehouse. As you emerge from the safety of your tunnel, make a right in between the crates.

Make another right and you should see a small barrel embedded in the crates. Walk past it and make another right.

You should see a guard with his back to you. Pop him one in the head. Now blow up that little barrel you just passed to find your Double Falcon 2.

Though this bottom floor may seem cleared, a few other guards may be roaming around. Carefully explore this floor and dispose of any straggling guards.

WARNING!

Watch for fire from above. If the guards on the catwalks above see you, they'll start firing. They'll even ride the elevator down to get you.

Grab the large elevator and head up. Keep your eyes open as you ascend. The guards sometimes wait for you on your way up. Shoot them before you reach the top.

When the door opens, make a right and target that lone doorman. The door behind him remains locked. Look in the Hidden Items section of this book to find out how to open it and what's behind it.

For now, go the other way, past the elevator you just came up on. Unless you attracted their attention when you were down below, there should be guards at this next door.

Through the door, you can see guards patrolling a catwalk above you. Snipe any that you can from here.

Make a left and wait by the elevator. When it comes down, it may be carrying some guards, so watch out.

PERFECT DARK

TIPS

Most of the guards will ride the elevator. A good trick is to set the secondary function on your Dragon and send it up with the elevator. When it comes back down, it should bring with it a pile of casualties.

Get on the elevator and check the top catwalk to make sure you've got all the guards. If so, it's time to head back. Go all the way back, down to where you started near that floating crate.

You may find that a few guards have appeared on your way back down. Wipe them out and grab your crate by pressing Reload while it is in front of you.

Bring it back to the catwalk at the very top. Follow it around until you reach its end. Look to your right and you'll notice an X scratched into the wall.

Drop the crate in front of the mark on the wall. Step back a few steps and shoot it until it blows. Your entrance is thus created.

NOTE

If the crate of explosives is destroyed before you reach the X, don't worry; you aren't doomed. Throw a Dragon in its secondary mode at the X and shoot it. The explosion will open the way for you. Or, if you were able to get the Phoenix, shoot the X with its secondary fire mode.

Through this hole is a series of tunnels. Turn left and go through a couple of doors until you reach an intersection.

Behind the right door stands a guard with his back to you. Pop him through the glass and pass through.

Be careful when walking through the next door. There is a biotechnician armed with Tranquilizers in here. If he hits you, you'll be in a daze, which makes it very difficult for you.

2 Shoot him before he hits you. From the door, turn to your left and activate the first red button you see.

2 This raises a containment unit directly opposite the button. Equip your X-Ray Scanner and take a look. Keep still for a few moments and you'll have completed a mission objective.

WARNING!

Always watch your back; guards can appear when you least expect them. There's nothing worse than getting capped for carelessness and wasting all that effort.

With this done, go back the way you came, past the hole you created. The tunnel begins to slant up and you reach another intersection.

Ignore these doors for now. Take a right and head down the slanted corridor. You approach two guarded doors. The one on the right is the one you're interested in.

mission 04

When you open the door, destroy the turret gun on your right as fast as you can. It won't shoot back at you right away. Notice the scientist running to a terminal to turn it on.

Shoot him down for his insolence. Don't worry about the other guy; he's now cowering in the corner. Instead, go to the terminal on the far wall, opposite where the gun was.

1 Upload a virus into this one with your Data Uplink. The virus unlocks a crucial door for you.

Exit this room and turn left. At the top of the tunnel, on your right, you find the door that was once locked.

walkthrough

1 Dispose of the two guards inside and go up to the terminal. Blow it to bits and an objective is completed.

Exit the room and turn left. Run down this corridor until you reach its end and a large metal door.

Notice the two smaller ones on either side. In Special Agent mode, go through the right door to find a scientist with your lab technician Disguise.

For now, carefully open the large door and prepare for a fight. A bunch of guards are to your left.

TIPS — After making your presence known, back up into the corridor and throw your Dragon in its secondary function at the door. When the guards swarm toward it, they'll go up in flames.

The safest way to rid yourself of them is to make your presence known, then immediately back into the corridor. From a higher vantage point, you can shoot them safely as you back up.

Go straight across this large room to the ramp. Up the ramp and along the catwalk, notice two walkways stretching across the room.

There's a break in the railing in front of the left walkway. Walk along it and duck down to fit through the ventilation duct.

When you drop down the first hole, you'll be in one of the labs. Walk straight ahead and through the opening at the end of the room.

Continue until you emerge into another room where you startle a scientist. To the right is a bunch of cabinets.

3 Knock out the scientist so he doesn't alert any guards. Now search through the cabinets and find the Disguise.

One minute and thirty seconds is all you have before the missing Disguise is noticed. Continue down this room and into the next. The narrow metal door on your left is your exit.

When you make it through, you should find this corridor very familiar. Take a left and run until you reach the top. At the top, take another left and run across the rubble you left when you made the hole.

3 At this point, put on the lab clothes and take the first door on the right. Get rid of any guards in here.

Before going through the door at the end of the room, put away your weapons. As you enter, you'll see another door with a glass viewing panel. Say "hi" to the ugly thug behind it.

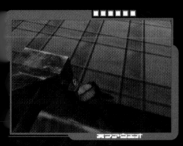

He's completely fooled by your ruse and lets you in. For his stupidity, introduce his teeth to your knuckles.

Now you can pull out your guns and shoot the scientist in the far right corner. Pick up his goods and enter the door to the lab.

TIPS After you shoot the scientist in the far right corner, turn around and throw your Dragon with its secondary function toward the door where you entered. This helps with the guards that are about to come through.

4 The scientist here holds a key you need. Do what you must to get it from him.

By now, more guards and biotechnicians should be coming in. Watch out for these guys; they have Tranquilizers that will daze and confuse you.

Make your way back to the main corridor and take a right. Enter the next door on the right with guns a-blazin'.

These guards are tough, so use the many obstacles around you to your advantage. Duck and weave, strafe and shoot.

At the far end of the room, you go through two more doors before entering a larger room. This room has many biotechnicians and guards, but one person here is your target.

In the far right corner of the room is a guard that holds the key to the operations room. If you hit him first, you can grab his key quickly and enter the lab.

mission 04

Interesting find, isn't it?

Co-Operative Notes

The guards in here are really tough. And with so many of them, splitting up is very dangerous. Stick together and make it easier on both of you.

Area S1–Escape

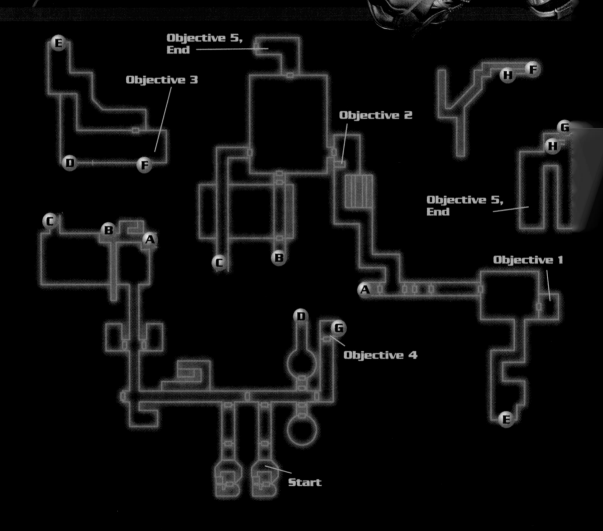

Objective 5, End

Objective 3

E

Objective 2

H F

G

H

D F

Objective 5, End

C

B A

Objective 1

C B

A

D

G

Objective 4

Start

E

Carrington//I know you have questions, Jo, and I'm afraid that this isn't the time to answe
tell you that the little fellow you just rescued is a Maian, and he is a bodyguard for the Ambass

OBJECTIVES

★ 1. Locate alien tech medpack

★ ★ ★ 2. Rendezvous with CI spy

★ ★ ★ 3. Locate secret hangar

★ ★ 4. Revive Maian bodyguard

★ ★ ★ 5. Escape from Area 51

Look for the numbers in the red-bordered screenshots in the walkthrough.
They indicate which objective is being accomplished.

★ AGENT ★ SPECIAL AGENT ★ PERFECT AGENT

What's all this green haze? Nerve gas. Better get the heck out of there. Now!

 TIPS

You can get a second Falcon and scope in the room behind you. Just let go of the alien and go get it. Be quick though; the nerve gas will start to affect you soon.

When you get to the corridor, take a right. Past the door, you find two biotechnicians who try to drug you. Just say no.

Take your alien through the brown door and left through the corridor. One more metal door and you'll be in the containment lab.

You are instructed to leave your friend and go find Jonathan. Head back the way you came until you reach the bodies of the biotechnicians you just blasted.

Go through the door on the right. Behind the next door are a couple more biotechnicians. Go around to the other side of the room to find a corridor that leads down to a metal door.

As you go through the door, turn right and shoot the guard in the far corner.

NOTE

If you were able to bring the alien to the containment lab within 38 seconds, you'll find a box of Remote Mines as you open the metal door.

While you're facing the guard you just shot, another guard comes into view from your left. In addition, the noise brings yet another guard through the door on the far end of the room.

Waste them. As you approach the door on your left, you'll find that you recognize the smell of this place. Go through the door and onto a metal walkway above a canyon.

Follow the walkway, taking out anything that crosses your path. You'll eventually reach another metal door.

1 In this next room, to your right, is a glass wall. Beyond it is a control panel you need to access. But your guns don't seem to affect it. Hmmm...if only there were something explosive nearby.

GNAL :STABLE

Well lookie here! An explosive barrel. Push this thing up against the glass and shoot at it until it blows. Problem solved.

1 With the glass gone, step up to the panel and activate it. It unlocks the door that holds the alien tech medpack.

Now to go get it. Go by the red light in this room and into the next area. Eliminate the guard there.

1 The first door you come across on your right is the one you just unlocked. Open it and grab the medpack within.

Turn around and go through the large metal door on the other side of the room. There are three more doors before you reach a T-intersection where you meet yet another guard.

Take a right and follow the hall until you reach a room with large mainframes around the edges. You meet two very unfriendly guards along the way. Don't let them slow you down.

2 Look in the left corner of this room to find Jonathan. Good, it looks like he's safe. Boy, aren't you glad you found him!

Right after your conversation with him, a bunch of guards come through the door. Launch a Grenade at them and watch them fly.

Go back the way you came, pausing at the T-intersection to Grenade the gang of guards through the door on the right.

Grab their goodies and continue backtracking all the way to the walkway above the canyon. Make sure you keep Jonathan in sight the whole time.

You encounter a few lone guards along the way. Blast them and move on. When you get to the end of the walkway, stop.

This is going to be fun. Four guards are on the other side of this door. They're clustered together, begging for a Grenade.

Prepare the Grenade Launcher function of your SuperDragon. Open the door and fire a Grenade at their feet. Was it as fun as you thought it would be?

3 When you get through the door, wait for Jonathan to come through. Once he does, he'll start preparing Explosives on the wall.

walkthrough

While he does that, your job is clear. Stand by the door leading to the catwalk and protect him from the oncoming guards.

Grenades work well against the guards on the walkway. They come in groups, so one Grenade can blow them away in a very efficient manner.

3 When Jonathan is finished, he'll take cover and you should too. The wall explodes, leaving a convenient hole for your escape.

Don't forget that guards are still on your tail. Carefully go through the hole while watching your back. There are also guards beyond the hole.

Head down the ramp and you'll notice a brown door right underneath the ramp. It's okay if Jonathan doesn't follow you right away.

Notice the HoverBike just sitting here.

4 Go through the brown door and you'll find your alien friend exactly where you left him. Administer the medpack and head back out to help Jonathan.

4 You have to hold off the enemies for a few seconds while the medpack finishes taking effect. When it does, return to the alien to find that he's about to wake.

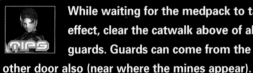

While waiting for the medpack to take effect, clear the catwalk above of all guards. Guards can come from the other door also (near where the mines appear). Use a Grenade to get them through the door. Either you or Jonathan need to come up here later, and it's best to have it empty when you do.

Whoa! He speaks English.

When the cutscene ends, return to the hangar and take a left at the end of the ramp. Make sure your two companions follow.

Stop near the flying saucer and wait for them. It looks like only two of you are going to be able to use it.

Jonathan volunteers to open the hangar doors and asks you to cover him.

5 You have two choices here. The easiest and fastest way out of this mission is to cover Jonathan. Follow him, but don't run in front of him until you reach the bottom of the ramp.

5 From here, you can lob Grenades into the hole and at the door under the ramp. This way, you'll protect both Jonathan and Elvis. Wait a few seconds and your mission is done.

Your second option is a little more challenging. If you follow Jonathan and walk in front of him toward the ramp, Joanna will offer to take care of the hangar doors for him.

There are two consoles on the catwalk above. Go up the ramp and use your Grenades to stop the first group of guards through the hole.

With them gone, you'll have a few seconds before another group comes. Follow the catwalk around until it splits.

S To the left is the console for the inner hangar door and to the right is the console for the outer door. Go ahead and activate them both. It doesn't matter in which order.

WARNING! While you are activating the consoles, keep an eye on your companions below. If the guards get to them while you're doing this, your mission fails.

With both consoles activated, Elvis and Jonathan are free to take off. How considerate!

S To heck with them. You can take care of yourself. Hop on the HoverBike by the ramp and arm yourself. You've got quite a ride ahead of you.

Go through the door underneath the ramp and hang a left.

Follow the corridor to the right when you get to the top. Speed on through the next few doors, taking out any guards on the way.

When you reach the top of this corridor, follow it down and right until you reach another door and a guard.

This door opens into familiar territory. Head to your left until you reach the end of this room. There will be a door on your right with more guards to greet you.

The hexagonal corridor leads across a bridge before it begins to slant up. Take it to the top and curve right.

The corridor opens into a room with slanted pillars. To your left, at the other end of the room, is an opening.

Walkthrough

You're almost there. Through the room on the other side of the opening is the last metal door you'll be going through in Area 51.

Open it up and cruise on through.

Co-Operative Notes

Teamwork is essential for this level. For the most part, the two players should stay close together. The guards here tend to come in groups that are best confronted with your partner.

You can split up while you're waiting for Jonathan to bust through the wall. One player can watch the door while the other watches the opening in the room. A few guards come through there after the explosion, so this keeps everyone safe.

While you run down the last ramp to administer the medpack, Jonathan usually stays at the top of the ramp fighting guards. Have the second player stay with him to make sure he doesn't get hurt.

When opting to open the hangar doors yourself, leave the second player with Jonathan and Elvis by the ship. They can protect them from any guards attempting to foil your escape. If a player beats Area 51—Escape by Hoverbike, Jonathan will be near Carrington's office in Carrington Institute—Defense.

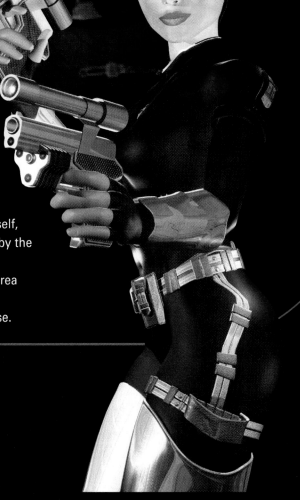

MISSION 04

MISSION 05

Air Base–Espionage

SIGNAL :STABLE perfect dark: program initiated...

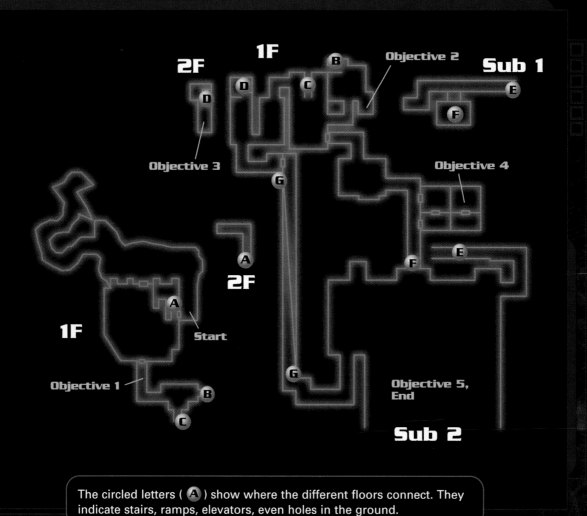

The circled letters (**A**) show where the different floors connect. They indicate stairs, ramps, elevators, even holes in the ground.

Background

Trent Easton has flown to meet the President at the air base in Alaska, preparing for the President's foreign visit. From the evidence gathered in Chicago, we assume that this is the start of his move against the President, and as such, it must be prevented.

Carrington// Care is needed here, Joanna. There are many innocent people about the air base. Only Trent's men or those strange blonde men are viable targets. Remember, the longer that you stay in disguise, the greater your chance of success.

PERFECT DARK

OBJECTIVES

★ ★ ★ 1. Obtain Disguise and enter base

★ ★ 2. Check in equipment

★ ★ ★ 3. Subvert security monitoring system

★ 4. Obtain flight plans from safe

★ ★ ★ 5. Board *Air Force One*

Look for the numbers in the red-bordered screenshots in the walkthrough.
They indicate which objective is being accomplished.

★ AGENT   ★ SPECIAL AGENT   ★ PERFECT AGENT

This mission starts outside, but before you can enter the building, you must acquire a Disguise. Take a couple of steps back and bring out your DrugSpy.

WARNING!

If you let a guard stand in front of you too long, he will shoot down your DrugSpy. This forces you to use your Crossbow and risk being shot at.

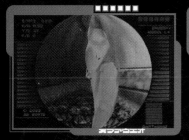

Use your DrugSpy to go around the corner of the building and shoot a drugged dart at the white guard by pressing your trigger. He instantly drops, slightly sedated.

Drug the rest of the white guards in this area. If another white guard sees one of his comrades fall, he will check out the scene, so dart him before he becomes too suspicious and runs to an alarm.

As you drop the guards one by one, the stewardess emerges from the tunnel near the cliff. Take your DrugSpy to her and dose her up as well.

1 As the woman falls, she drops her outfit. Take your DrugSpy down the tunnel to take out the remaining white guards. Then have Joanna collect the dropped objects including the uniform.

Run down to the end of the tunnel to get the Proximity Mine on the left side of the ledge. Be sure to pick up the dropped weapons and your DrugSpy on the way.

1 Return to the front of the main door and select the Disguise from your inventory to put it on. Make sure you are unarmed before entering.

After entering the room, hang a left and take the elevator up. The elevator takes you to the room containing the suitcase.

Arm yourself with your Crossbow as you enter the room. You must sedate both of these guys before they run for security. Once they are down, take the suitcase from the far end of the room.

1 Remember to unarm yourself and have your Disguise on as you return downstairs. Take the double doors to complete Objective 1. That part wasn't so hard, but don't get too comfortable.

mission 09

walkthrough

2 Walk forward down the escalator. To your right is a metal detector down the hallway and to the left of the hallway is a baggage conveyor. Go to the conveyer belt and place your suitcase on the platform by equipping it and pressing Ⓑ.

You now have 30 seconds to shut down the security monitoring system. Run through the metal detectors and follow the hall into the large room with the other escalator.

On the floor are colored lines. Follow the blue line into a hallway with pillars on the right side. Follow this around and make a right past the next hallway.

You should be facing a hallway with a flight of stairs at the end. Take the stairs up to a room with a terminal and two guards.

3 Immediately disarm the guard in the dark coat and turn to activate the terminal. Once the security system is deactivated, turn and take down the guard in the dark coat.

WARNING! The guard in white begins to fire at you if the guard in the dark coat did not shoot him. Remember, you cannot shoot him. Either punch him or run.

Now you're in for some trouble. With the security system shut down, all the guards in the building are alerted and after you. Go downstairs and get ready for a fight.

At the bottom of the stairs, you face a mess of guards. Use your new weapon to mow them down. Use the stairs as cover and to reload.

When you have a clear hallway, take a trip back to the room with the escalator going up. In this room, go to the door to the right of the hallway leading to the metal detectors.

Follow the green line to the room with marble floors. Go down the left hallway and follow the orange line to the first door on your left.

This man tells you that someone is trying to steal from the safe. The safe must be near. Go through the door next to the man's desk.

6 5 6 5 6 6 5 6 6 5 4   2 1 0   2   0 0 1 2   2 1 0 0 0 0 1
4 4 4 4 4 4 4 5 4 4   4 5 6 5 6   5 6 7 6 6 4 4   4 6

Take a left through the busted door. On the left of this room is a door with a mine on it. Shoot the mine from a distance to shatter the window next to the door.

4 Climb through the window and go to the back right corner of the room. Press Ⓑ on the panel to move the cover and Ⓑ again to press the switch to open the safe.

4 Jackpot! The safe is open and ready for you to take its contents. The flight plans are yours. Now it's time to board the plane.

Head back out the window and straight through the two busted doors into the room with the orange and purple lines. Follow the purple line into the elevator.

This elevator takes you all the way down to the hangar level. Don't exit the elevator when it opens. Activate the elevator again to go up a level.

5 Exit the elevator and go left. Follow the hallway around into the docking shuttle that will take you to *Air Force One*. Strap on your wings and get ready to fly.

If your Disguise is no longer active, take the elevator back up and head toward the room with the escalator going up.

Follow the blue line again toward the security monitoring system. Follow the hallway with pillars to another hallway on the left.

Take this hallway to a cargo elevator. Watch out for the guard hiding around the corner next to the door. Take the cargo elevator to the bottom.

Once you leave the lift, follow the hallway to a panel on your right. Shoot the panel until it blows up. This overloads the laser grid.

Take this hallway into the hangar and look at the lasers on your right. They are fading in and out. Carefully follow the path of broken lasers.

Once you have made your way through the maze of pulsating lasers, climb up the ladder under the nose of the plane. Pack your bags and get ready for your trip.

mission 05

Co-Operative Notes

Both players start on the side of the building. One player can use his DrugSpy to sedate all of the white guards and the stewardess. He can then put on the uniform, grab the suitcase, and deactivate the security system. Once the security system is down, come back and let the other player into the double doors. From this point you can join forces to finish the mission.

Air Force One-Antiterrorism

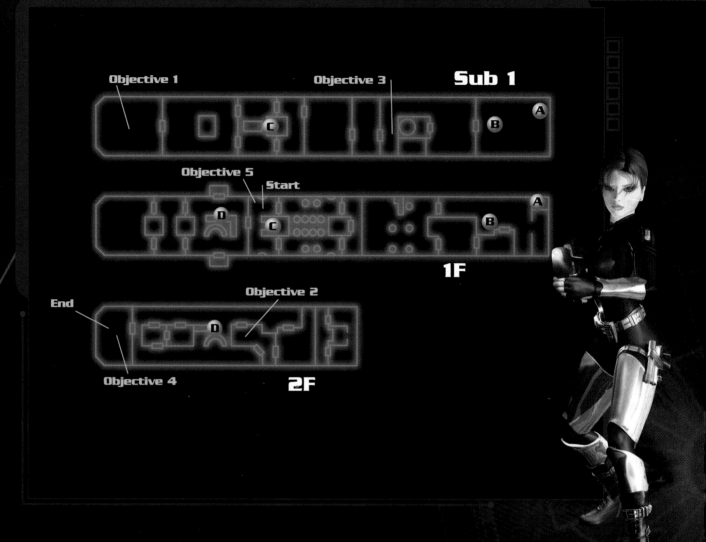

Objective 1   Objective 3   **Sub 1**

A
B
C

Objective 5
Start
D
C
A
B

1F

Objective 2
End
D
Objective 4

2F

Background

Trent Easton's plan to abduct the President is in motion. The Carrington Institute response hinges on removing the President from *Air Force One* before Trent can do the same.

Carrington//

Time is short, Joanna. In order to foil Trent's plan, you have to get the President off the plane. That means convincing him of Trent's betrayal, which in turn means getting the evidence from the baggage hold and showing it to the President.

OBJECTIVES

★ ★ 1. Locate and retrieve equipment

★ ★ ★ 2. Locate President

★ ★ ★ 3. Get President to escape capsule

★ 4. Secure *Air Force One* flight path

★ ★ ★ 5. Detach UFO from *Air Force One*

Look for the numbers in the red-bordered screenshots in the walkthrough. They indicate which objective is being accomplished.

★ AGENT   ★ SPECIAL AGENT   ★ PERFECT AGENT

PERFECT DARK

NOTE If you entered the plane through the ladder under the nose in the previous level, you will start in the cargo hold in the belly of the plane. If you entered through the docking shuttle, you will start in a hallway at the top of a small service elevator.

NOTE If you used the ladder to enter *Air Force One* in the last level, skip to Objective 1 and follow the walkthrough from there.

WARNING! Remember, you cannot shoot the President's guards. If you pull out a gun, they will attempt to shoot you. If this happens, punch them. Do not return fire.

You are now a stewardess on *Air Force One*. Your objectives are clear, so let's find the evidence. Go through the door you are facing, past the guards, and into the door on your left.

Take the next two doors on the left. After entering the second door, turn right near the end of the hall and notice the red grate on the floor. Press ⓑ to open it.

Take the revealed stairs down and through the door. Travel through the next four doors until you reach a kitchen with two other flight attendants.

These flight attendants know you are not one of them, so you must quickly knock them down before they can find security.

Continue in the direction you were heading, into a cargo room containing a HoverBike. Pass the craft and go into another cargo room with a guard. Disarm him and drop him with a knuckle to the head.

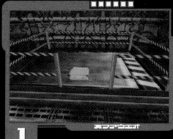

1 Pick up the key card he drops. Push the red button on the left wall and collect the case from the cargo lift.

Now that you have the evidence, you need to find the President. But first, return to the room with the hovercraft and use your key card to activate the red button between the two doors.

Go back into the kitchen and press ⓑ on the small terminal in the alcove between the doors. This gives you access to the small service elevator next to it. Hop inside.

You arrive in the room where you started. Head through the decorated door in front of you and up the stairs. (Setting up a Laptop Sentry above this door is helpful.) You are notified that the President is on this level.

WARNING! The guards in this room may want to shoot at you now. If you must, disarm them. Otherwise, avoid them and find the President.

mission 09

2 From the top of the stairs, make a right and enter the room to your right guarded by a soldier. The President is alarmed by your presence, but agrees to follow you to the escape pod.

With the President on your side, his guards will no longer be a problem. However, Trent's guards in black are fair game. Shoot away and do anything to protect the President.

Guard the President as you make your way back downstairs to where you started this mission. There is a gray umbilical connector under the exit sign.

WARNING!

The plane is now filled with many of Trent's guards. Be sure to watch your back as well as the President's. Guards will come from behind, so watch all directions.

5 Throw a Timed Mine at the end of the umbilical connector. This will detach the UFO from *Air Force One*. Turn and run as if your life depended on it; it does. Objective 5 is complete.

Uh oh! The pilots have died. You need to make your way to the cockpit, so go through the decorated door and up the stairs. Make a right at the top of the stairs.

Waste the guard in front of you and go through the next two doors. Shoot the two guards in the cockpit.

4 Between the two pilot seats in the cockpit, there is a flashing red button that needs your tender touch. With the flight path secured, Objective 4 is complete.

Now, get the President off the plane. Make your way downstairs and toward the red gate you went to earlier.

Use the Combat Boost now. Once you reach the last room with rows of chairs, just before the red grate, Trent and two of his blonde thugs will confront you.

Use the door to block some gunfire and focus on taking out Trent's guards. Trent runs off laughing as his guards fall to your bullets.

MIPS

There's no need to fire at Trent. He only runs off. If you do catch him, you cannot dispose of him. Instead, he follows you around incessantly.

3

Continue to the red grate. Once you enter the red grate, go through the door in front of you. The President knows what to do from here. He runs into the escape capsule, completing Objective 3.

Co-Operative Notes

This mission is best to run through together. After getting the President, have one player guard his back while the other takes the front. When the time comes to place your mine, have the other player run ahead to the cockpit. Between the two of you, this mission will be over in a jiffy.

Crash Site-Confrontation

Objective 3

Objective 4

Objective 5,
End

A

A

E B

E C

B

D

Objective 5

E C

B

D

Start

Objective 2

Objective 1

mission 09

Background

Following Elvis's last-ditch maneuver, the three craft involved have crashed close together in the Alaskan wilderness. The whereabouts of the President are uncertain, and a cloud of ECM jamming is preventing rescuers from finding the site of the crash.

Carrington// At this moment in time, this one-way text messaging system is the only way we can communicate with you, Joanna. If you can remove the source of the jamming then we can get a fix on your location and send help. But locating and ensuring safety of the President should be your most important task.

OBJECTIVES

★ ★ 1. Retrieve Presidential medical scanner

★ ★ ★ 2. Activate distress beacon

★ 3. Shut down enemy jamming device

★ ★ ★ 4. Retire Presidential clone

★ ★ ★ 5. Locate and rescue President

Look for the numbers in the red-bordered screenshots in the walkthrough.
They indicate which objective is being accomplished.

★ AGENT   ★ SPECIAL AGENT   ★ PERFECT AGENT

This area is big and difficult, but you're a Perfect Agent right? Start your journey forward, keeping the mountainous wall to your right until you reach two guards facing away from you.

TIPS If you turn around from where you start and travel a short way down, you'll find the HoverBike. It's there only if you remembered to push the red button near it on *Air Force One*. The HoverBike is good for covering ground fast, but poor for trying to shoot from the top of it. You may want to get off of it before engaging in any gun activity.

Sneak to pistol range behind the guard on the right and cap him in the head. Do the same to his partner on the left. Collect their guns and head to the escape pod to your far left.

2 On one side of the escape pod is a red button. Push it to activate the distress beacon. Objective 2 is complete.

Before you can find the President you need to find his medical scanner. Return to the spot where you shot the first guard. Take the pathway next to his body.

Walk down the path, keeping the wall to your right until you come across a couple of lamps lying on the ground.

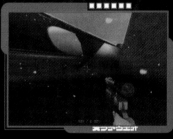

From here you can see a blonde guard near the side of the downed airplane. Creep up behind him and gun him down. Take the Sniper Rifle he leaves behind.

Hike up to the nose of the plane and take out the guard standing on the ledge in front of you. Look slightly to the right to see a suitcase lying in the snow.

1 Walk down and grab the case. This is the presidential medical scanner. Select this from your items menu to get a radar in the top right corner of your screen.

NOTE There are two red dots on the presidential scanner. One indicates the real President and one indicates the impostor. There is no way to tell the dots apart.

From the suitcase, walk to your right around the large rock near the plane wing. Shoot the guard hiding here.

Follow the ledge in front of you toward one of the guards you shot earlier. Continue walking along the ledge and up the path you are heading toward.

Keep the wall to your right until you reach the escape pod. From the escape pod, you can snipe a few guards on patrol to the right of the plateau.

WARNING! If the guards catch on to you here and begin to fire back, move away from the escape pod. Otherwise, stray bullets could make it explode, causing your mission to fail.

With the guards out of your way, continue with the wall on your right and turn down the first path you come across.

Make your way down this path past the piano and around the first corner. Use your Sniper Rifle to shoot down the guards wandering around in the distance.

Walk to the end of this path by following the ridge. Pass the first walkway on your right and the airplane tire to reach a narrow walkway.

You can shoot more guards from this ledge. Step down on this path and walk through the tunnel. A large clearing with trees is at the end.

Slow down as you come to the end of the tunnel. Two turret guns are waiting to unload if they see you. At the end of the tunnel, grab your K7 Avenger.

Zoom in on the base of the third tree from the left. One of the turret guns is there. Shoot it down. Be careful not to step out of the tunnel or the other gun will fire.

MISSION 05

From the same spot at the end of the tunnel, face right and sidestep to shoot the second turret gun.

Use the wall of the tunnel to hide. When you hear the firing stop, pop out and shoot at the turret gun again. Do this a few times to blow it up.

Now go toward the second turret you blew up. Down the hill to your left are two guards and the enemy spaceship that is emitting the ECM jam.

3 Show the guards your bullets and walk up to the craft. Place a Remote Mine on each of the wings and the nose, then run back. Detonate them to complete Objective 3.

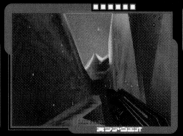

Now backtrack a little. Make your way back through the tunnel you came in and up the walkway.

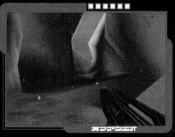

Take a right just before the airplane tire. At the fork, make a left followed by a right, down the green-and-white trail.

Take this through a tunnel and into a clearing with a large hole in the center. Take care of the four guards here.

From the trail, shoot one guard and pick off the other three as they squeeze through the opening to shoot you.

4 Walk to the edge of the hole and look down. Below is a man that looks a lot like the President, but is it? Of course it's not—the President was wearing a jacket. Put a bullet in his head with the Sniper Rifle.

A few guards run to the fallen impostor's side. Take them out too. Now let's find the real President.

Backtrack your way to the airplane tire. From the tire, head down the tunnel to your right. Some guards may try to stop you on the way.

From inside the cave, turn left. Follow this down until you come across an opening on the wall to your right. Look down to spy a flying robot with guns. Take him out with a round or two from your K7 Avenger.

These flying robots are pushed back when they are struck by gunfire. Try to shoot them into each other so when one blows up, the others blow up too.

PERFECT DARK

Continue to your right past the small ice tunnel on your left. You come across the remaining three flying robots (four if you were unable to get the one earlier). Destroy these before going on.

After you have taken out the flying robots, continue down the path. As soon as you enter an opening, turn to your right to see the President and Trent.

S Immediately shoot at Trent until he runs off. If you wait too long to shoot, Trent will shoot the President. The President is now in your custody.

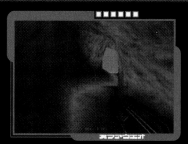

With the President behind you, go back to the small ice tunnel you passed earlier. Take the tunnel to the surface.

NOTE
Remember that you are now responsible for the President's safety. Watch his back as well as your own.

From the end of the tunnel, run slightly to your right toward the group of red rocks in the distance. On the other side of them is Elvis's ship.

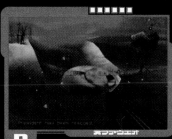

S Take the President to Elvis and he will take care of him. This completes your final objective.

Co-Operative Notes

To utilize both players effectively, have one activate the distress beacon and grab the presidential medical scanner while the other player blows up the enemy craft and takes out the President clone. Both players should meet up at the tunnel near the airplane tire to rescue the President. This makes it easier to dispose of the flying robots and escort the President safely to Elvis.

mission 09

MISSION 06

Pelagic II–Exploration

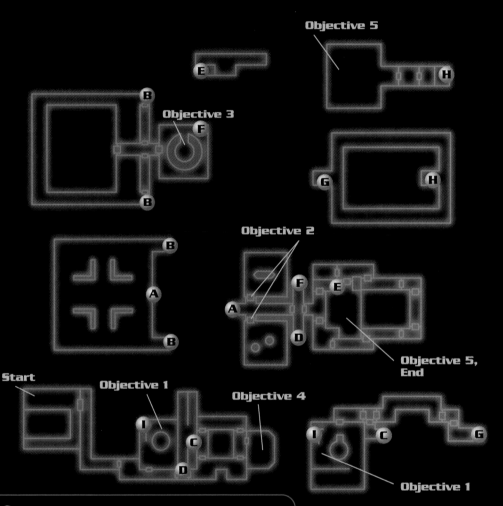

Objective 5

Objective 3

Objective 2

Objective 5, End

Start

Objective 1

Objective 4

Objective 1

The circled letters (A) show where the different floors connect. They indicate stairs, ramps, elevators, even holes in the ground.

Background

The conspirators have thrown caution to the winds and have committed an act of piracy, taking over the *Pelagic II* and commencing hurried diving operations in the Pacific Ocean. Both dataDyne and its strange allies are involved in what appears to be a joint operation.

Carrington//Although this move seems reckless, it only serves to highlight how important the operation on the seabed must be to dataDyne and its allies. Disrupt the operation as extensively as possible, but remember our minimum force rules for noncombatants.

16655365656665 210 12 0012 21000001

OBJECTIVES

★ ★ ★ 1. Disable primary power source

★ 2. Secure laboratories and research data

★ ★ ★ 3. Deactivate GPS and autopilot

★ ★ 4. Activate Moon Pool lift

★ ★ ★ 5. Rendezvous and escape with Elvis

Look for the numbers in the red-bordered screenshots in the walkthrough.
They indicate which objective is being accomplished.

★ AGENT   ★ SPECIAL AGENT   ★ PERFECT AGENT

Walk to the left side of the door in front of you. Peek through the window at the guard. Line up your sights on the man's head. Open the door and fire.

Turn right down this corridor until you near the end. Turn to your left and crouch to see a guard around this corner. If you're careful, he won't see you as you put a shot into his head.

If he does see you, he will run to activate the black screen on the wall across from you, setting off the alarm. Shoot him before he can get to it.

NOTE

Try everything in your power to stop the alarm from sounding. If a guard activates an alarm, many guards will come for you. To stop an alarm, press Ⓑ at the black screen.

With the guard taken care of, walk to the window of the next door. Shoot the guard in the head through the glass.

One of his good buddies will come to his side as the guard falls. Aim through the glass and shoot his friend in the head too.

Now open the door and walk up to the wall in front of you. Slowly sidestep to your right until you see the body of another guard. Blast him as quietly as possible.

Stop any guards from activating the alarm to your right or throw a Laptop Sentry Gun out and around the corner. Once the hallway appears to be clear, open the door on your left.

On the other side of the wall in front of you is a security camera. Circle around the wall until you can see the tip of the camera. Two shots should take out this threat.

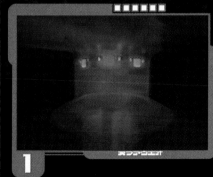

Now turn to the large circular power generator. Take out your X-Ray Scanner. Pretty cool, huh? Activate the green screens placed around the cylinder by pressing Ⓑ.

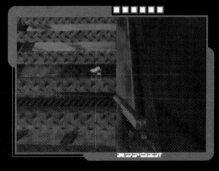

When all the green screens have been turned black, turn off your X-Ray Scanner and walk halfway down the stairs. Turn and face the stairs to see another camera.

mission 06

1

Walkthrough

1 Position yourself to take out the camera. It's time to flip the switch on this thing. Head to the protruding cylinder opposite the door. Push that little green button. Objective 1 is complete.

Make your way back up the stairs and through the door you came in. Go left down this hall and open the door. Take a left up these steps.

Open the first door on your left in this hallway. There is a camera on your right side. Shoot it down from the doorway. Now enter the hallway and make a left into the first door you cross.

2 Disarm yourself before opening this door. Once you open the door, two scientists come running for the door. Knock them out before they can leave this room.

2 As they drop at your feet, they each leave you a research data disk. Leave this room and cross the hall to smack one more scientist. You have secured the laboratories and research data, completing Objective 2.

Make a left from the room containing the last scientist. Go out the door and hang another left toward the green-lit stairs. Shoot the two guards at the top of the stairs.

You can shoot these two guards from the bottom of the stairs to avoid getting shot at.

3 Take the next flight of stairs up to a control room. Run up to one of the control men and stick your gun in his ear. He quickly agrees to pull the plug.

3 While he is tinkering with the terminals, watch the other two men. One of them decides to pull out a gun and take out his coworkers. Pistol whip or kill this fool and collect his Magnum.

3 Now that the men know you are serious, turn back to the man you gave orders to earlier. He will now shut down the terminals completely. Exit back down the stairs you came up.

Take the stairs all the way down. Make a left into the first door you come to. Pop out and shoot the guard to your left, then turn around and enter the door beyond the blue crates.

A guard is behind each crate on your left. Be a little sneaky to shoot them with minimum gunfire. Sidestep to get them into your sights without them seeing you.

Walk to the blue door to the left of the second guard. Shoot the two guards in the next hallway through the window of this door.

PERFECT DARK

The guards in these hallways are not the brightest. Shoot them through windows whenever possible. They don't have enough sense to shoot back.

Pass through the blue door at the end of the hallway. Be careful; the guards in this room will shoot the crates, causing them to explode, so don't stand too close. Use the door for cover if you need to.

When you have taken out the two guards, travel to the end of the hallway and peek through the window. Another poor sap is waiting for a bullet in his head.

Go to the next door and look through this window as well. Do these guys ever learn? Wreck shop through the window.

Go down the hallway, collecting dropped ammo, and open the next door. Make a left and shoot some more guards through the window. Go to the next door when you're finished.

Through this door are two guards to your left. Strafe from the boxes and shoot these men down. Take the door to your left in this hallway.

Walk into the large room with a railing around water. To the left is a terminal on the wall. Activate it to unlock and open the lift door.

4 Go through the large door and down the ramp to your right. At the bottom of the ramp is a terminal. Press it to activate the lift and complete Objective 4.

Okay, time to find Elvis. Go to the door under the large lift door. Stand to the left of the door when you open it to get a free headshot at the guard here.

Lots of guards come running into this hallway. Toss in your Sentry Gun and take a step back. Shut the door to prevent the guards from coming after you.

WARNING! If you enter this door and then exit back into the large room with the lift terminal, guards will jump out from boxes and fire at you. Stay close to the outside of the door to shoot the guards if your Sentry does not take them all out. These guards spawn when the alarm sounds. If no alarm is set off, guards never appear in this room.

Once the gunfire has subsided, go through the door and make a right. Enter this door and quickly shoot the guards to your left before they can activate the alarm next to you.

Go through the door at the end of this hall. Make your first right down a flight of stairs. You can shoot both guards on patrol here from the top of the stairs.

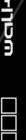

Enter the door near the bottom of the steps. Take the door on your right. Around the corner of this hallway is a guard under a security camera. Creep around the corner until you have a clear shot at the guard.

Prevent this guard from hailing help by shooting him in the head. Take out the camera above him before it sees you. An alarm will sound if the camera catches you.

Go to the end of this hallway and through a door. Go through the next door on your right and follow the hall to a set of stairs leading down.

At the bottom of the steps are guards to your left and right, so stand at the top of the steps and fire a few shots down to get their attention.

Shoot the guards as they walk by and as they try to come up the stairs. When it seems all the guards have fallen, walk down the stairs and go left.

NOTE

There are six guards down the stairs, however two of them may stay guarding the entrance to the second set of stairs.

Follow this path around to another set of stairs. Two guards may be on post here. Take them out. Walk down the stairs. There are two more guards on post here. Shoot them from the top of the steps for a safer fight. You can use your Sentry Laptop to help.

S Shoot the next guard through the window and go through the next set of doors. Behind the last door you will reunite with Elvis.

S Elvis orders you to follow him. Now the easy part: follow Elvis' skinny little booty to the water area with the railing. He takes a familiar path, but most of the guards have respawned.

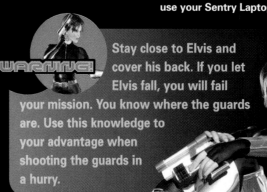

WARNING!

Stay close to Elvis and cover his back. If you let Elvis fall, you will fail your mission. You know where the guards are. Use this knowledge to your advantage when shooting the guards in a hurry.

S When you have reached the end of your journey, Elvis climbs down the small ladder. Join him to complete Objective 5.

Co-Operative Notes

The best way to do this is to start off together and shut down the primary power source. Have one player beat up the scientists and secure research data while the other player deactivates the GPS and autopilot. Meet up together in the long hallways on your way to activate the Moon Pool lift. Together, rendezvous with Elvis. Between the two of you, getting Elvis to safety should be no problem.

WALKTHROUGH

Deep Sea-Nullify Threat

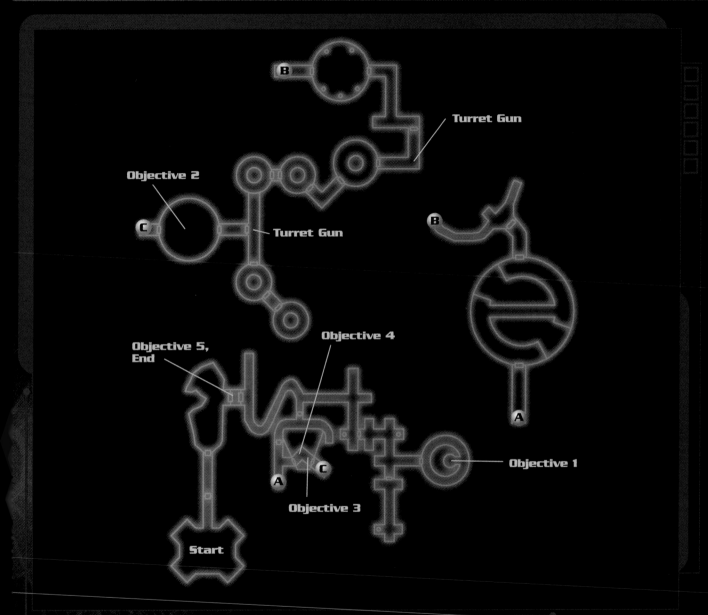

- B
- Turret Gun
- Objective 2
- C
- Turret Gun
- B
- Objective 4
- Objective 5, End
- A
- A
- C
- Objective 1
- Objective 3
- Start

mission 09

Background

The goal of this conspiracy is revealed at last—a massive alien ship lies on the floor of the Pacific. At least partially sentient, though sleeping, the Cetan Ship is even now being overrun by the Skedar and their unwitting minion, the dataDyne Corporation.

Carrington//Our cursory examination of the research data astounds us. We've put together as many objectives as we can based on our interpretation of this data. The massive structure on the sea floor is a spacecraft of alien origin. It is apparently a sentient craft, of a race called the Cetans, though it is currently dormant. However, it houses the most

OBJECTIVES

★ ★ ★ 1. Reactivate teleportals

★ ★ ★ 2. Disable Cetan megaweapon

★ ★ 3. Secure control room

★ 4. Restore Dr. Caroll's personality

★ ★ ★ 5. Escape from Cetan Ship

Look for the numbers in the red-bordered screenshots in the walkthrough.
They indicate which objective is being accomplished.

★ AGENT ★ SPECIAL AGENT ★ PERFECT AGENT

walkthrough

TIPS

Elvis has a better arsenal than you do, so let him do most of the dirty work. Lead him near enemies to make him shoot them, while at the same time strafing to avoid fire. This saves you time and effort.

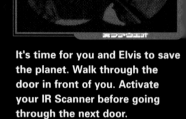

It's time for you and Elvis to save the planet. Walk through the door in front of you. Activate your IR Scanner before going through the next door.

With the IR Scanner, you can see the cloaked guards in this room. Clear this room and head to the hallway on your right. Open the next two doors.

Four more cloaked guards are here. Once they are gone, turn off your IR Scanner. Take the corridor to your right and blast the three guards near the end.

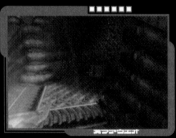

Make a left into the tunnel. Shoot the guard on your way down and make a right at the intersection. At the top of the small hill, turn to your right and shoot the block on the floor.

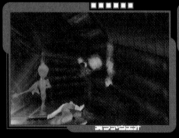

This causes the block to light up and open the door behind you. Turn around immediately and strafe to the side, letting Elvis shoot a majority of the guards.

When the hallway is clear, walk forward to the next block sitting on the floor. Shoot it to open the door on your right. This releases another guard, but Elvis will chase him down.

Walk straight down this hallway until it ends. There is one more block on your right just before the dead end. Shoot it and backtrack two intersections. Make a right and head for the open door.

Time to reactivate those teleportals.

1 Through the door are three guards. Shoot them from the door opening. Once you and Elvis have cleared the room, Elvis operates the control panel that reactivates the teleportals.

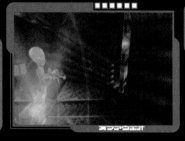

Head out of the room and make a right at the first intersection, followed by a left at the bottom of the small hill. Run down this hallway to the green block on the floor, then make a right.

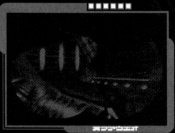

At the next intersection are two cloaked guards. Take out your IR Scanner and let Elvis help you take them down. Go up the pathway they were protecting. You are now near...

Open the door to your left and take the corridor on your right. Follow this around to another door. From here, run straight into the gelatinous wall.

6 6 5 5 6 6 5 6 5 6 5 | 2 1 0 | 2 | 0 0 1 2 | 2 1 0 0 0 0 0 1
4 4 6 4 6 6 5 5 | 4 5 6 5 6 5 6 7 6 5 4 4 5

NOTE

In Agent mode, the teleport warps you to a series of long tunnels. Escort Elvis to the room containing a terminal and cover him from little Skedars while he completes Objective 2.

In Special Agent mode, the warp takes you to a path similar to the one for Perfect Agent. In Special Agent mode, however, you venture down a spiral pathway to a room in which you must stand behind Elvis and protect him from Skedars while he sabotages the megaweapon terminal.

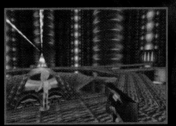

Whew. That was fun. Elvis now hands over his FarSight. From this hallway, use the Target Location function of the FarSight to clear out the men in the next room.

Take this door into the circular room. Make your way to the other side by walking over the large pipe connecting the two sides.

Go through the next set of doors and run into another teleporter to your left. Open the door in front of you and shoot out the five green glowing tubes. When all the tubes have been shattered, the door across the room will unlock.

WARNING!

To avoid the little Skedars dropping from the vents, shoot the green tube from outside the room using the Farsight.

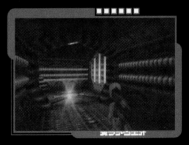

Run across the room and through the door. Make a right at the end of this hall. Watch out for little Skedars along the way. Make a left at the next hallway. Follow this around to a door on your right.

Down this hallway is a turret gun placed on the top of the second arch. Shoot it from a distance with your Falcon 2 and continue down the hallway. Take a right at the end of the hall and slide through the next door.

Through this door is a green tube in the center of a room surrounded by little Skedars. Blast away at the tube until it breaks. You can rely on Elvis to shoot most of the Skedars.

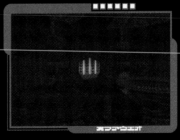

Run through the door across the room and follow the hallway to another door. Open the next door and blast another large tube, then enter the door it unlocks.

There is another turret gun on the top of the second arch. Blow it up and follow the hallway to the door ahead of you, passing the door on your right. Open the door and shatter another green tube. Do this again for the next room you come to.

MISSION 06

| 2 | 1 | 0 | 1 | 1 | 1 | 2 | | | 2 | | 4 | | | 4 | 5 | 5 | 5 | 5 | 6 | 5 | 6 | 5 | 6 | 5 | 6 | 5 | 6 |
| 2 | 1 | 0 | 1 | 1 | 2 | | 2 | | 2 | 2 | | 3 | | | 4 | 5 | 5 | 4 | 6 | 4 | 5 | 4 | 5 | 4 | 5 | 4 |

walkthrough

Take the door across the room into a Skedar-filled hallway. Brave your way through with Elvis at your side. Go through the next door and blast the last green tube.

Now return to the door you passed earlier. It is now open, revealing a tunnel with a door at the end. Stand against the door and use your FarSight to shoot the turret gun on the ceiling of the next room.

2 With the turret gun gone, it is now safe to enter. Walk into the bare room and bring out your FarSight again. Aim at the red cylinder between the two bright lights to your left and right, and fire.

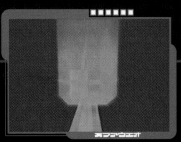

Once both cylinders have exploded, the door will unlock. Enter this door to another teleport.

3 Bust out your handy dandy FarSight once again and gun down the two soldiers on guard in the next room. You have just secured the control room. Way to go!

4 Enter the control room to find Dr. Caroll. Open your inventory by pressing (START) and select your backup disk. When you exit the menu, you slide the disk into Dr. Caroll.

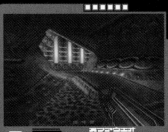

5 After the cutscene, you have 60 seconds to exit the Cetan ship. Go through the door on your right and follow the hallway around until you can make a left.

Go through this door and run past the guards. Follow this hallway all the way around until you come across a blue corridor on your left.

 Don't waste time shooting guards on your way out of the Cetan ship. Just use your crafty dodging skills to pass them by on your way out of this underwater time bomb.

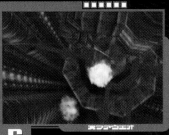

5 Just two more doors to go and you're home free. Now sit back and enjoy the show as the Cetan ship explodes behind you.

Co-Operative Notes

Elvis follows player 1, so have player 2 cover player 1 and Elvis. Player 2 should also be on Skedar patrol making sure they don't threaten Elvis or player 1. The key here is to just watch each other's backs, while making sure Elvis goes unharmed.

MISSION 07

Carrington Institute—Defense

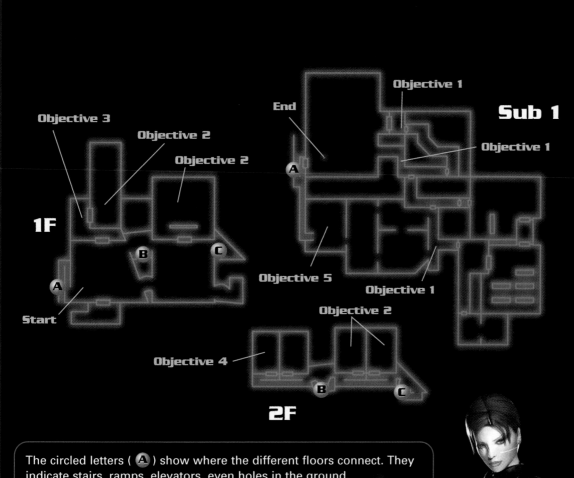

The circled letters (A) show where the different floors connect. They indicate stairs, ramps, elevators, even holes in the ground.

Background

In revenge for the foiling of their grand plan, the Skedar have attacked the source of their troubles, the Carrington Institute. With an organized response out of the question, it falls to Joanna to save what she can of the Institute from total destruction.

Carrington//They've caught us completely off guard, Jo! Save who and what you can, then get out yourself. After all, the Institute is the people, not the building.

OBJECTIVES

★★ 1. Reactivate automatic defenses

★★★ 2. Release hostages

★★★ 3. Retrieve experimental weapon

★ 4. Destroy sensitive information

★★★ 5. Deactivate bomb

Look for the numbers in the red-bordered screenshots in the walkthrough. They indicate which objective is being accomplished.

★ AGENT ★ SPECIAL AGENT ★ PERFECT AGENT

walkthrough

Turn to your left and dispose of the Skedar. Then Carrington tells you about the need to get the automatic defenses back online. Turn around and run down the ramps. Take the hallway that lies in front of you at the bottom of the ramp.

At the end of this hallway, make a left and run across the helipad to the door slightly to your right. Run across another helipad and through another door on your right.

The guards in this level have Shield technology, making them harder to take down. Use automatic weapons for faster results.

1 Cross this room into the door in front of you. To your right is one of the guns you must reactivate. Head to your left and make your first right. Here on the corner is one of the terminals for the guns. Press Ⓑ to activate it.

Do not stand in between a guard and an automatic gun. The automatic gun will shoot you in attempt to take down the enemy. Lead enemies to the gun, but stay out of gunfire.

Go back into the hallway to the right of the terminal and make a right. Head past the stacked crates and enter the blue double doors in front of you. Make a left down this hall and follow it to a blue door.

1 To your left is another automatic gun and a terminal. Head that way and look on the wall to the right of the automatic gun for the terminal. Activate it and return to the hallway to the right of the terminal.

1 Run past the stacked crates and through the double doors at the end of the hallway. Follow this path around through the door under an automatic gun. On your left is the last of the terminals you need to activate.

Now go up the small set of stairs in this room and out the door. Follow the metal walkway around the aircraft to a blue door on the other side of the building.

Head to your left and make your first right. Go up the series of ramps. From the top of the ramp, go left into the Institute lobby.

It's time to save the hostages. Make a left toward the wall and then run to your right until you reach the second elevator on you right. Take this elevator upstairs.

Make a left off the elevator to the first door on your right. Use a Combat Boost here. Switch to your AR34 or K7 Avenger as soon as the Boost has been initiated.

2 Open the door and shoot the guard in front of you, then quickly turn to your right and shoot a second guard. Be careful not to harm the hostages. Once these hostages are free, exit this room.

TIPS Your Boost does not last long, so you must hurry through these hostage situations without harming innocent people.

2 Now circle around the partition to your right and make a right into the next room. Open this door and take out the guard in front of you.

2 Turn to your left and aim for the guard here. The female hostage runs in front of you; use your dynamite marksmanship to shoot the guard behind her without putting a bullet into her back.

There are still some more hostages to save. Run back to the elevator you used earlier and go back downstairs. Make a left and go to the first door on your right.

NOTE If a hostage dies, continue. One or two hostages lost will not cause you to fail your objective unless you shoot them.

2 Take another Combat Boost here. Enter the door and go right. Round the corner and quickly turn to your left. Open fire on the line of guards shooting at the hostages. When they have all fallen, exit the door and go to your right.

2 Go into the next door you come across to your right. A hostage in here is fighting with a guard. Help him out and put a bullet into the guard. This completes Objective 2.

3 Carrington now tells you of an experimental weapon that you must retrieve. It just happens to be in this room. Walk over and activate the terminal to open the glass protecting the weapon.

Use your new weapon on the guards that join you in this room. Exit the room and go left. Hop in the elevator to your right and take a ride upstairs. You need to visit Carrington's office.

At the top of the elevator, go all the way to your left and enter the door here. Walk to the back left corner of the room to the metal slab on the wall. Bring out your laser and place a steady stream on

Watch your back when trying to open the safe. Many guards try to stop you from destroying an item that they would love to possess.

4 After a few seconds the wall breaks, revealing Carrington's sensitive data. Destroy the data with the laser and return to the elevator to go downstairs.

NOTE
If you escaped Area 51—Escape by Hoverbike, Jonathan will appear outside Carrington's office. He'll help guard you as you open the safe.

Now you only have two minutes to deactivate the bomb on the Skedar craft, so you have to hurry. A few blonde guards want to stop you. Use your new weapon to blast them down.

TIPS
It is not always necessary to shoot down every guard when running to the Skedar craft. Shoot guards along the way, but never stop running for the ship if you are getting low on time.

Run back to the ramps where you started and make your way down. Make a right at the bottom of the ramps. At the end of this hallway make a left onto the helipad.

5 Here you find the Skedar craft. Bring out your Data Uplink and activate it next to the ship. Strafe to dodge any fire while you upload the virus to deactivate the bomb.

Once Objective 5 is complete, waste any guards shooting at you and exit the door you just came

Co-Operative Notes

In this mission, you can have one player activate the automatic defenses, while the other player starts saving hostages. Or you can simply work together through each objective. Once the hostages are free, both players should go to Carrington's office. One player can destroy the sensitive material while the other player watches the door for guards. Do the same for deactivating the bomb. Because of the high number of guards, you'll need to cover each other well in this mission.

walkthrough

PERFECT DARK

MISSION 08

Attack Ship–Covert Assault

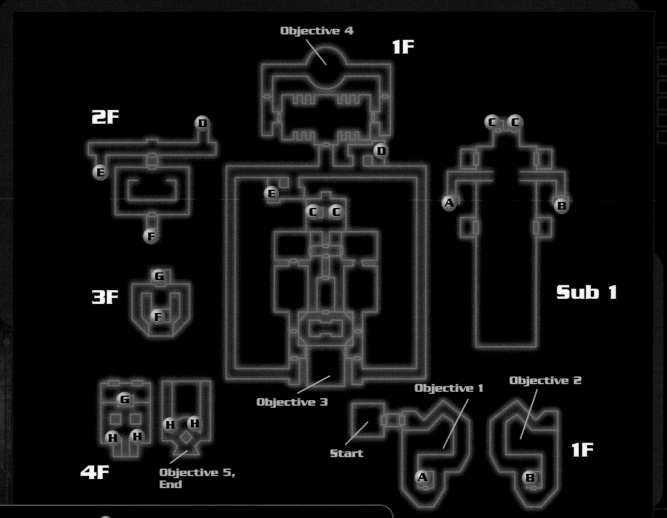

Objective 4

1F

2F

D

E

D

E

C C

C C

A

B

3F

G

F

G

F

Sub 1

Objective 3

Objective 1

Objective 2

G

H H

H H

Start

A

B

1F

4F

Objective 5, End

The circled letters (**A**) show where the different floors connect. They indicate stairs, ramps, elevators, even holes in the ground.

Background

Knocked unconscious during the evacuation of the Carrington Institute, Joanna wakes to find herself a prisoner aboard a Skedar assault ship.

Carrington//Not Available

Elvis//Joanna! I'm following the assault ship that is holding you! With me are two Maian protectors from the delegation at the White House. If you can get us aboard, we can help you take over the ship.

| 2 | 1 | 0 | 1 | 1 | 2 | | | | 2 | | 4 | | 4 | 5 | 5 | 5 | 5 | 5 | 6 | 5 | 6 | 6 | 6 | 5 | 6 | 6 | 6 |
| 2 | 1 | 0 | 1 | 1 | 2 | | | 2 | | 2 | 2 | | | 4 | 5 | 4 | 5 | 4 | 5 | 4 | 5 | 4 | 5 | 4 | 5 | 4 | 5 |

OBJECTIVES

★ ★ ★ 1. Disable shield system

★ 2. Open hangar doors

★ ★ ★ 3. Access navigational systems

★ ★ 4. Sabotage engine systems

★ ★ ★ 5. Gain control of bridge

Look for the numbers in the red-bordered screenshots in the walkthrough.
They indicate which objective is being accomplished.

★ AGENT ★ SPECIAL AGENT ★ PERFECT AGENT

Once again, you've gotten yourself in quite a pickle. The only weapon you have is your trusty Combat Knife. How were you able to smuggle that thing in here wearing only your dinner dress?

Equip the Poison Knife feature of the Combat Knife and head out the door in front of you.

You hear Cassandra's scream as you pass through. There are two Skedars in this area. If you arrived here quickly enough, you'll just catch one of them running up the ramp on the other side of the room.

The other Skedar has its back to you. For the most part, it won't move too much. Stay on this side of the room and flick your Poison Knife at it. Aim carefully—you don't want to fight these guys with your bare hands.

Quickly grab the Skedar's Mauler. Don't forget about the Skedar you saw running up the ramp. That guy is hiding around the corner. Use your newly-acquired Mauler on it.

WARNING! Be sure your aim is up to par for this level. Ammo is scarce and you've got a long way to go. Using the Charge-Up Shot on your Mauler takes six shots—five to charge and the sixth to fire the blast. If you miss, you're in trouble. Pick up every piece of ammo you see.

1 Walk past the elevators for now and descend down the ramp until you see three strange-looking panels. These control the ship's shields. Destroy them and you've got the first objective in the bag.

Time to take the elevator down to the next floor. Walk down the hallway until it turns left. Peek around the corner and up the ramp. You notice a Skedar on patrol.

Take careful aim with your charged-up Mauler and fire at it. Another Skedar roams around up there. If they see you before you get your shot off, lead them back down the ramp where you'll have more cover.

After eliminating them, run straight across to the opposite ramp leading down. Make a left when the tunnel does and hop on the elevator. When you get off, go around to your left and you'll meet yet another Skedar.

2 Get rid of it and use the ramp to access the lower level. This time, there are only two funny-looking terminals. Activate the one on the left to open the hangar.

With the hangar open, Elvis is able to meet you at the bottom of the elevator. And to show his appreciation, he brought you a present. The AR34 is a great weapon—use it wisely.

Follow the path back up the ramp that leads to the hangar. The two Skedars in here look eager to be targets for your new weapon. The large doors by the ship also open and reveal a few more Skedars.

NOTE You can shoot the two Maian guards in here with no penalty and take their Callistos. It's mean, considering they've been helping you shoot the Skedars, but you need the weapons more than they do.

After you've rid yourself of these vile things, Elvis tells you to jump on one elevator while he uses the other. Do as he says and use the left one. You emerge in a room with a door and a window that looks out into space.

Through the egg-shaped door, you find two Skedars, one on either side. Dispose of them and enter this next area.

You've reached a four-way intersection. Take the left door and enter a room with what looks like a small table. To your right is another egg-shaped door.

The door opens into a hallway with lighted pillars. Behind the last of the pillars is another Skedar. Use the pillars for cover and blast away.

NOTE Though Elvis does help you with the enemies, don't let it soften you. Elvis will drop if you start to slack off. Protect him at all costs.

Go through the door on the other side of this hallway. It leads into another hallway with a door farther down. As you go down this hallway, angle yourself to the right. It's really easy to miss this turnoff.

Take this turnoff and you'll reach another door. The navigational systems behind this door are crucial to your mission.

After you open the door, you see two Skedars waiting for you on your left. Pop in and out of the doorway to safely clear this room of them.

If Elvis isn't in the room with you yet, wait a few moments. When he arrives, he'll access the navigational systems for you.

Exit the same door you entered through and take a right. Through the next door is a dark hallway and a Skedar. Blow it to bits and press forward.

3

mission 08

SIGNAL STABLE

Follow the corridor up the ramp. The corridor turns left at the top and then turns left again a little way down. You'll meet a couple of Skedars along the way, so keep on your toes.

Eventually, on your right, you reach another ramp that leads up. Walk past this for now and into a room with a circular floor.

To your right is a blue egg-shaped door. This leads into a dark room with two more blue egg-shaped doors, one on either side. Take good care of the Skedar scurrying around in here before moving on.

You can go through either door here because they both lead to the same place: the engine room. A bunch of Skedars patrol this area and the hallways that lead to it. Take your time and dispose of them as safely as you can.

4 The engine room is pretty impressive, no? Too bad it's your job to sabotage it. Look up at the brightly-lit tube and notice the two gold plates holding it up.

Aim your weapons at them and fire until they're gone. Now get out of there before that thing blows.

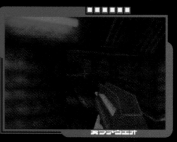

Head back to the room with the circular floor. Take a left and then another quick left. You should now be heading up the ramp you passed up earlier.

Follow the corridor around until you reach another circular floor. Go left through the door and prepare yourself for a tough battle.

Beyond the next door are two Skedars posted on catwalks. The best way to deal with these wise guys is to peek in, say "hello," and back out. Let them come after you and you'll have an easier time disposing of them.

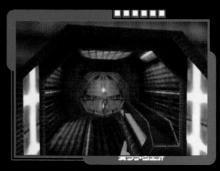

When you finally do, take either catwalk up to the door at the top. Go through the door. The next door you find is an elevator. Take it up to an empty room that leads to yet another elevator.

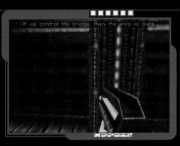

Tired of doors and elevators yet? Well, this is your last one. When you get into the elevator, don't turn around to face the doors. Stay facing the wall.

When you reach the top, you have reached the bridge. Three Skedars await you, so immediately fire off a few shots while you back up and take cover.

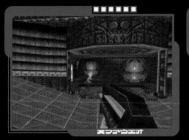

Take them out as quickly as you can. They'll try to hunt you down before long, so it's best to beat them to the punch. When they're finally gone, Elvis will appear from one of the doors behind you.

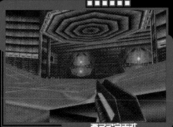

He's going to need some time to take over the bridge. It's up to you to cover him while he does. Take a position on either side of the ramps and keep an eye on the doors.

You have your work cut out for you. It is utterly important not to let any of the Skedars reach Elvis. If they do, you'll have a hard time killing them without hitting Elvis.

Buy him enough time and Elvis will capture the bridge. Excellent work, Jo.

Co-Operative Notes

This is a great level for teamwork. Because the Skedars often come from different directions, you can divide the labor very efficiently.

When clearing the hangar, have each player watch opposite sides. The doors open on either side, releasing vicious Skedars. Stand back-to-back and protect each other.

Up on the bridge, have each player guard a different door. Decide beforehand who will chase any Skedars that manage to break through. This way, you avoid both players chasing one Skedar and leaving the doors open.

MISSION 09

SIGNAL : STABLE

Skedar Ruins–Battle Shrine

walkthrough

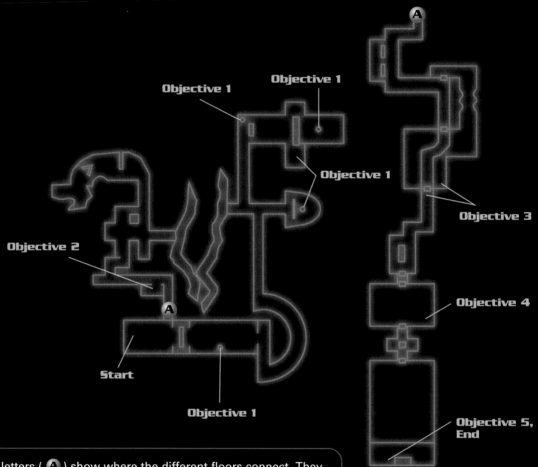

The circled letters (Ⓐ) show where the different floors connect. They indicate stairs, ramps, elevators, even holes in the ground.

Background

The hidden heart of the Skedar religion is exposed at last—a desert planet burning under three suns. The leader of the Skedar terrorist faction is based at the Battle Shrine on the surface of the planet. The destruction of the Shrine and the death of their leader would break the morale of the Skedar.

Carrington//Not Available

Elvis//There's some groundwork to do, Joanna—I need parts of the temple marked as targets for bombardment. And we need to be absolutely certain that the Skedar leader is dead. He is sure to have powerful shielding capable of withstanding gunfire, so you may need to destroy part of the

OBJECTIVES

★ ★ ★ 1. Identify temple targets

★ ★ ★ 2. Activate bridge

　★ ★ 3. Gain access to Inner Sanctum

　　★ 4. Destroy secret Skedar army

★ ★ ★ 5. Assassinate Skedar leader

Look for the numbers in the red-bordered screenshots in the walkthrough.
They indicate which objective is being accomplished.

★ AGENT　★ SPECIAL AGENT　★ PERFECT AGENT

NOTE
Time to kick some Skedar butt. These buggers are as tough as they are ugly. Add cloaking ability and you've got one formidable opponent.

First things first. Elvis has requested that you target three obelisks for bombardment. Pull out your R-Tracker to help you find where they are.

NOTE
The R-Tracker brings up a circular HUD in the upper right corner of the screen. Though it tells you where your targets are, it doesn't show you the obstacles or walls in the way. You usually cannot head straight toward it.

TIPS
Your Callisto NTG is more powerful than your Falcon. That's exactly why you want to use your Falcon when you can. Save the Callisto ammo for later, tougher opponents. Open areas such as this are perfect for the Falcon because you can back up while shooting.

You start this level in a seemingly peaceful courtyard. Go through the opening in front of you to find someone who disrupts the serentity.

If you lure it back into the courtyard, you'll have room to maneuver while plugging it with slugs. Use your Falcon even though it'll take quite a few shots to down it.

Move through the opening and around the partition; pause before you walk in front of the opening on the other side. Crouch down and slowly peek through the opening: another Skedar.

It's oblivious to your presence. Position yourself so that you can just target it, using the wall as a partial shield. Now quickly fill it with lead from your Falcon. This one returns your fire, so duck in and out if you need to reload.

As you enter this next room, a cloaked Skedar makes its presence known. This one won't shoot at you but it will chase you. Use run-and-shoot tactics to take it down.

NOTE
There are five of these tall, slender structures throughout this level. Three of them are your targets. Which three? They change every time you run through it. We'll show you how to get to all of them, but it's up to you to use your R-Tracker to decide if the one in front of you is an actual target.

MISSION 09

1 In this room you find your first obelisk. Move toward it and watch your R-Tracker. If the yellow dot merges with the green dot, throw one of your Target Amplifiers onto it.

Move through the opening on the far side of the room. Follow it right, then left and into a semicircular path.

When you move a little way down this path, a Skedar appears behind you. Turn around and backpedal down the path. This way, it'll appear in front of you and you can shoot it before it even becomes fully uncloaked.

WARNING! If you have to maneuver a bit to kill the thing, don't move too far along the path. There's another Skedar up ahead and you don't want to prematurely alert it to your presence.

Face forward again. About midway down the path, you see another Skedar. Dodge and weave as you put it out of its misery.

As you approach the end of the semi-circular path, another Skedar appears. Usually it's to your right, down the next path. Not always though, so watch your back.

This next path leads to a T-intersection. Now's a good time to pull out your Callisto. Two Skedars are here, one on either side of the T.

Poke your head out and start firing at one while you back up down the path you came in on. Use the length of the path behind you to your advantage. The suckers follow and you can pelt them with your High Impact Shells.

WARNING! When pulling these backing-up maneuvers, make sure you know what's behind you. There's nothing worse than backing into a pillar or corner when you have one of these deadly beasts charging you.

1 With them gone, take a right at the T. You'll enter a cul-de-sac with a wall and an obelisk in the middle. Is this one of the obelisks you're looking for? If so, throw your Amplifier on it and head back toward the T.

Walk past it and take a right at the next intersection. Down at the end of this path is a Skedar. This bad boy's got a weapon, but yours is bigger.

Walk down toward the freshly created corpse and find another obelisk. Don't go to it just yet, though.

The opening to your right reveals two Reaper-wielding Skedars. Shoot them before approaching the obelisk. Slap an Amplifier on it if you need to.

Venture into the room where you just shot the Skedars. Past where they stood is an opening you want to go through.

1 Take a right and go up the stairs. My! What a large obelisk you have!

Head toward the stairs opposite these and stop just as you reach the bottom steps. Look to your right and notice a small opening.

In Agent mode you'll find a Shield at the top of the second set of stairs.

1 Be careful when you go through this one because two Skedars guard the last obelisk. Destroy them so that you can safely place your Target Amplifier. You can also throw the Amplifier onto the pillar without entering the room.

With all that out of the way, it's time to exit the way you came. Past the stairs and the two dead Skedars, turn left. Then, make a right at the intersection.

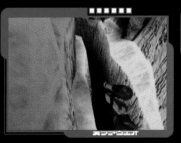

Uh oh. Who took the bridge? Carefully step to the edge and look down and to the left. Notice the path on the other side of the chasm.

It seems to end suddenly at a square outcropping. On the other side of this outcropping, still on the ledge, is a Skedar. Set your Devastator to Wall Hugger mode and aim at the outcropping. You want it to land high on the side facing the chasm and toward the Skedar.

In Agent mode, there is no outcropping. You just see a Skedar waiting for you.

If you've done this correctly, you'll be looking at a cleared ledge: no outcropping and no Skedar.

Now for some fancy footwork. Step as close to the edge here as you can. There is a narrow ledge below you on this side of the chasm. To get to it, turn left and carefully take a step forward or simply gun it and strafe/jump across.

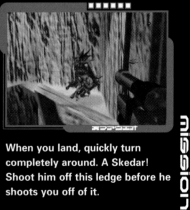

When you land, quickly turn completely around. A Skedar! Shoot him off this ledge before he shoots you off of it.

Turn back around so that the wall is immediately to your left. Follow it until you reach a small drop-off. Don't worry, it's a short fall. Step off and continue around.

When you come to a point where the ledge on the other side of the chasm meets the ledge on this side, step across.

mission 09

walkthrough

To your right are some steps grooved in the wall. Use these to climb up to the higher ledge. Does this look familiar?

This is where you shot your Wall Hugger earlier. Walk right past it and turn around to your left. Climb these grooves in the wall to reach stable ground again.

At the end of this hallway, you come to a short ledge. Hop down and catch the Skedar on your left off guard. Start shooting him before he fully materializes. Once he does, he'll be on the move and you're his target.

From where you stepped off the ledge, walk straight ahead until you come to a wall. Turn left and you'll see a really short dead end. Or is it?

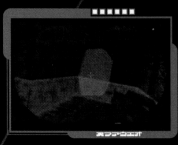

Slap on your IR Scanner and check it out. Notice the discoloration on the wall. Another Wall Hugger serves you well here.

Through the hole begins a series of tunnels. Follow the tunnel right and then left. Pause here and wait for a couple of smaller Skedars to attack you.

TIPS If you like, you can use your Falcon on these little Skedars. They take a couple of shots to destroy, but you save your more powerful Callisto ammo for more powerful opponents.

Drop down the short step and head left. As you approach the door on your right, watch out for the steady stream of Skedars from the end of the hallway.

Though they seem endless, they aren't. When they're all gone, carefully open that door on your right. If it jams, try it again. A small and rambunctious fellow greets you.

Do what you like with him and take a look around. Not much in here, huh? Just a missing tile on the floor with a funny pattern.

There's also what looks like a slab of concrete sitting here with a funny pattern on the top. Wait a minute...could it be?

2 Push the concrete slab until it slides into the missing tile space. Now look across the ravine. Notice the bridge that just slid across it.

Exit through the door and veer right. Cross the bridge but pause before it gets too dark. You need to take care of the oncoming Skedar first.

Equip your IR Scanner and venture forth. Push forward until you reach a door on your left and a ramp on your right.

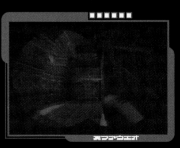

Watch out for the few Skedars coming down the ramp. Leave the door for now and go up the ramp. Another door awaits you at the top.

The door opens to a bridge that stretches across a very dangerous room. On either side of you, down below, are Slayer-bearing Skedars.

These stupid things won't see you until you start shooting at them. Pick either lucky Skedar and position yourself in the doorway. Line up your shots and fire a few bursts as fast as you can.

Don't wait around too long. Strafe to safety before you can see the smoke trail coming at you. Repeat this for both sides until the two Skedars have been exterminated.

Continue along the bridge and blast the Skedar guarding the door. Hmmm… The door is locked.

Drop off the bridge and go directly underneath the door. Notice the two green lights above a little altar.

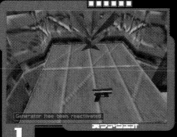

1 A sacrifice to the God of War is requested. Place one of your weapons on this altar and it will unlock the door above. Equip the weapon you want to sacrifice and tap Reload (Ⓑ) to place it. Make sure you're looking straight down at the altar.

NONE

You can place any weapon on the altar except the Reaper.

TIPS

If you have any Grenades left coming into this room, use them on the Rocket Launcher Skedars. By the time you get to this altar, your Devastator will be out of ammo and you can sacrifice it to get through the door.

Run around to the other end of this room to find the door. Through the door is the ramp that leads back to the bridge.

3 The door that was locked earlier is now open. Pass through it and experience the Inner Sanctum. Follow the path until you reach a set of doors immediately followed by another set.

Get your guns ready because the secret Skedar army is in suspended animation behind these doors. There are seven of them, each in its own capsule.

Luckily for you, the Skedars won't all thaw at once. This diagram shows from where and in what order these guys come at you.

TIPS Use the Callisto's secondary function to shoot the Skedar through doors.

Now that you know the order they appear, simply be there when their doors open and greet them with the muzzle of your gun.

With the Skedar army defeated, go through the door on the other side of the room. Catch your breath in this small area before moving on.

This is it. The Skedar leader is in this next room. Ready your weapons—this is going to be a doozy.

Beating the Skedar Leader

The leader of the Skedar is highly shielded and is armed with a variant of the Rocket Launcher—his scepter launches rockets. Sitting upon its platform, it can summon lesser Skedars to do its dirty work. In addition, when it's feeling feisty, it can teleport down to your level and rock you hand-to-hand. How, then, do you beat it and save the world?

So you've noticed the Skedar leader is shielded, but did you notice the Shrine behind it glows as though it were shielded too?

It turns out that the Skedar's shield draws its power from the Shrine. When you first hit the Skedar, its shielding is red. As you damage it more, it turns yellow and then green. To recharge itself, it'll stop and draw energy from the Shrine.

When you enter the room, position yourself a little past the halfway point. This is a good position because it gives you plenty of time to dodge the rockets by strafing. This is the best way to dodge because you can keep your eye on your opponent.

Persistence is key here. Keep pecking away at the Skedar until its Shields turn green. When this happens, it'll rest in the middle of the platform, charging its Shields.

While the Skedar is charging you can actually do some damage—not to the Skedar, but to the Shrine behind it. Notice the yellow Shields around the smaller spikes; they're gone.

Aim your weapons at these unshielded spikes. A decent amount of gunfire makes them drop. You're not going to be able to get all of them before the Skedar is finished charging so be prepared to repeat what you just did.

Occasionally, the Skedar raises its arms. That means it's summoning a lesser Skedar. Watch one of the front corners near the platform because that's where they spawn.

When the Skedar teleports to the lower area where you are, there's really nothing you can do but run away. Shoot at it some more so that when it returns to the platform, it'll be ready to charge.

When all the little spikes at the bottom of the Shrine are gone, the next Skedar charge will take down the main spike's Shields. Unload anything you've been saving on this last spike.

Finally! Victory is yours.

Co-Operative Notes

The Skedars on this level are really tough. It's possible to split up to plant the Amplifiers but we don't recommend it. Staying alive so you can encounter the leader is the priority here.

The rest of the level is really linear. Splitting up doesn't make much sense—you're weaker and you have no one to watch your back. Stick to the buddy system for this one.

walkthrough

SPECIAL ASSIGNMENTS

. Blonde's Revenge

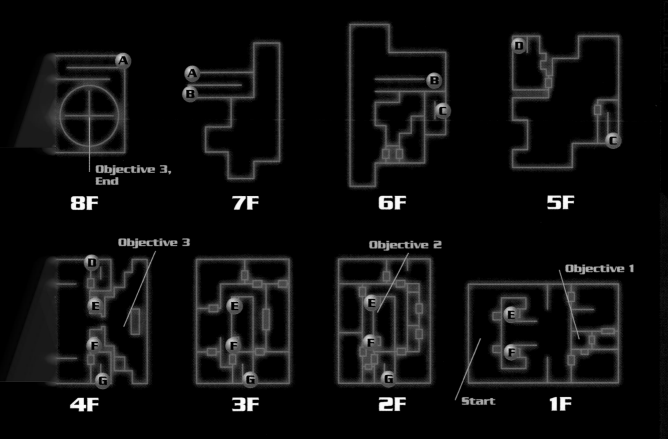

8F — Objective 3, End

7F

6F

5F

4F — Objective 3

3F

2F — Objective 2

1F — Objective 1, Start

he circled letters (**A**) show where the different floors connect. They dicate stairs, ramps, elevators, even holes in the ground.

ground

mpetent Cassandra De Vries of the human ion dataDyne has obstructed the Skedar cause enough. Enter her headquarters and capture at she may be brought before righteous Skedar

OBJECTIVES

★ ★ 1. Plant explosive device in lab lift

★ 2. Eliminate dataDyne Captain

★ ★ ★ 3. Locate and escort Cassandra to helipad

Look for the numbers in the red-bordered screenshots in the walkthrough.
They indicate which objective is being accomplished.

★ AGENT ★ SPECIAL AGENT ★ PERFECT AGENT

walkthrough

As soon as the mission starts, head around behind the reception desk and pick up the two CMP150s. Then switch on the Cloaking Device. As you face the doors you came through, head to your right.

Do not shoot anyone yet. When you see the stairs to your right, go to the left, into an alcove with a desk and a door.

Go through the door and past the guards to see the elevator with the dataDyne symbol on it. That's the lab lift where you'll eventually use the Skedar Bomb.

NOTE

It is imperative not to let one of the guards get between you and the elevator. She will lock the doors and you won't be able to plant the Skedar Bomb—Objective 1.

Now turn and fire on the guards. Use the doorway as cover and make every shot count. One of the guards has double CMP150s, so don't slack off.

NOTE

On Perfect Agent difficulty, these guards are good enough to warrant your highest skills. You must have high accuracy rates. But by now, you probably do.

When the fighting dies down, venture into the area you just cleared. Do not plant the Skedar Bomb yet.

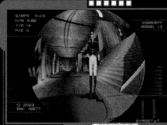

Stand near the door that leads to the elevator and launch the BombSpy. Fly it back out to the lobby area with the stairs.

TIPS

Ammo is at a premium in Perfect Agent difficulty. Strategic use of the BombSpy helps you save bullets.

Lure guards past the stairs and to the door by the couch. Open the door.

Three guards follow the BombSpy out to the lobby. Try to cluster the guards together and then trigger the bomb.

NOTE

The BombSpy tactic has to be employed rather quickly. Eventually the guards wise up and disable the BombSpy.

Gather ammo and then go out the door to the alcove with the desk. Peek around the corner and see how many guards are left.

Take out the rest of them—again making your shots count—then collect ammo and walk up the stairs. Make sure that the entire first floor is clear of guards.

As you walk up the stairs, head to the right. Face the small elevator door and press Ⓑ to call the elevator down. You're not setting the Skedar Bomb yet because the countdown is a mere four minutes.

Get on the small elevator and ride it up until it's disabled. You're trapped as the other lift rises to meet you. Shoot out the glass now so your shots at the captain aren't impeded.

6 6 6 5 5 6 6 5 6 5 8 6 5 2 1 0 0 0 1 2 2 1 0 0 0 0 0 1
4 5 4 5 4 5 4 5 4 5 5 4 4 5 0 6 6 5 6 7 6 5 4 5

NOTE

For Agent difficulty, ride back down, and call and get into the elevator the dataDyne Captain was in. Ride it up until it stops, press Ⓑ, and ride it up one more floor to the level with Cassandra's office.

2 The dataDyne Captain is going to try to take care of you herself. Aim down and fire as her lift gets close, following it as it comes up. Once she's dead, your second objective is complete and your lift begins to rise again.

As soon as the lift stops, press Ⓑ and ride it *back down* to the lobby. Trust us on this one.

1 Once you are back in the lobby, head to the lab elevator and place the Skedar Bomb on the back wall. You now have four minutes to get Cassandra and get out.

NOTE

The elevator may already have come down with an angry guard inside. Be prepared to shoot or dodge around her and into the elevator.

Now go back to the two small elevators at the top of the stairs. Call the one that the dataDyne Captain was in—the one to the left as you go up the stairs.

Ride up. When you stop, you'll most likely have a gaggle of trigger-happy guards waiting. Shoot at them, but don't leave the elevator. When you get a chance, get near the door and press Ⓑ to close it.

The elevator rises one more floor. Just to your right is Cassandra De Vries's office. Just in front of you is a helmeted guard with a Magnum. Drop him.

Tread carefully now; there are guards in the stairwells to either side of Cassandra's office. Some of them have N-Bombs that will be the death of you. As you approach Ms. De Vries's office, one pops out of the stairwell door. Cap him before he can throw his N-Bomb.

Put away your guns and change your attack to Disarm. Enter Cassandra's office. The lady is not happy to see you. Run around the desk and take her pistol from her.

Turn your attention to the office doorway and clear it of enemies—if they've shown up. Do not shoot Cassandra, who may flee from the office as you're dealing with the guards.

Ms. De Vries follows the path to the roof and your helicopter, but she'll take her own sweet time unless you're behind her to prod her along. Get her going and then run ahead of her up the stairwell to your right as you exit the office.

When you reach the room at the top of the stairwell, stay ahead of Cassandra again and take aim at the guards on the ramp. Blast them quickly or they'll ruin your day with another N-Bomb.

3 Persuade De Vries to climb the final ramp to the helicopter.

Jump aboard and congratulate yourself. You've captured the vile human and destroyed her building.

Co-Operative Notes

The best thing about having two people in this mission is two BombSpies. Follow along the same path for the first bit—cloaking and running to the lab elevator. Send the first BombSpy on the first floor guards as per usual. Stay together until you get to Cassandra De Vries's office. Then send one player in to pick up the lady while the other goes up to clear the path. Alternately, have one player stay at the lab elevator to make sure it doesn't get locked, while the second player *really* clears out your opponents from the path to the roof.

Maian S.O.S.

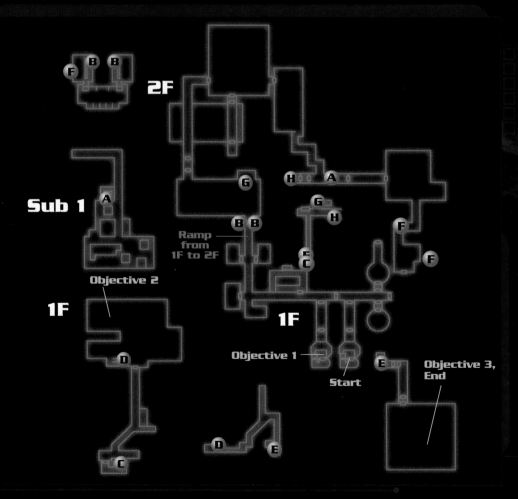

2F

F B B

Sub 1 · A

G H A

Objective 2

1F

D

C

Ramp from 1F to 2F

B B

G H

G

E C

F

F

1F

Objective 1

Start

D E

E

Objective 3, End

Background

Emergency capture protocols activated. Ship XD-310372 suffered hostile planetfall. Maian Protector One (Aelphaeis Mangarae) sole survivor. Planet designated pre-contact status; paranoia grade 'B+,' intolerance grade 'B,' xenophobia grade 'A.' Destroy equipment remaining; prevent examination of Maian technology and/or personnel.

OBJECTIVES

★ ★ 1. Sabotage enemy medical experiment

★ 2. Destroy captured Maian saucer

★ ★ ★ 3. Activate distress signal

Look for the numbers in the red-bordered screenshots in the walkthrough. They indicate which objective is being accomplished.

★ AGENT   ★ SPECIAL AGENT   ★ PERFECT AGENT

NOTE: This mission has no time limit, but it has very limited ammo and a lot of enemies. Take the time to lure and Disarm guards as often as you can. If you're low on Dragon ammo, consider using the Proximity Mine function on a group of guards.

Walk over to the lab technician and let him notice you. He pulls out a Falcon 2. Disarm him as soon as you see the gun.

Go to the door and run through. A second technician is there with a Falcon 2. Disarm him as well and pick up the Psychosis Gun on the desk.

WARNING! If the technicians raise their hands or run out the door, they're no longer a threat. They may pull out another gun, however, so keep an eye on them. Actually, this can be a good thing because you can Disarm them again and get more ammo.

Bump the hover bed over to the big glass windows and back away. Fire shots into the bed until it explodes, smashing the glass and freeing you from the medical lab.

This next bit is tricky. Switch to Disarm and head to the doors facing the med lab. Stand in the center of the doors, open them, rush forward, and Disarm the guard in the alcove. Knock him out, if you can, but make sure the door behind him opens.

Duck back through the door and take cover at the side. Switch to the Dragon, set it for Proximity Self Destruct, and toss it into the alcove.

WARNING! There's a chance you won't get all the guards in the blast so stay sharp.

SPECIAL ASSIGNMENTS

walkthrough

Move down the hall and out the far door. A guard patrols this larger hall but may be behind one of the doors. If he's visible, make him chase you and then duck back into the first hall.

Wait by the side and Disarm or shoot the guard when he comes through.

As with the other missions, Perfect Agent level requires extremely accurate and quick shooting. Also, when using the Disarm move, time it so that the guard is reloading when you charge.

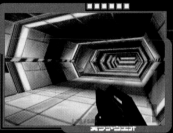

More guards may respond to the ruckus—give them the Proximity Mine treatment if they do. Exit the first hall and turn to your left. Go through the large door and then through the smaller door on the left.

TIPS If you go to the right, you'll find several guards in front of two doors. You can risk injury to deal with them and then find the guard with Double Magnums. Use the Psychosis Gun on him and you'll have a powerful ally—until he gets gunned down. Try it and decide if the trouble is worth it.

This hall is identical to the first one you came across except four guards sit at desks on either side of the walkway. Sneak in and headshot them one by one. Use single shots to take out the guards. Blasting away just alerts the others.

Go through the doors at the end of the hall and you'll find another medical lab. This one has two technicians and the body of a Maian on a hover bed. Make your way into the lab.

1 Beware of the technicians, they have Tranquilizers—one of them occasionally drops a Psychosis Gun. Knock them out and then fire at the hover bed until it explodes. That takes care of the first objective.

Make your way back to the main hallway and turn left. The hall turns to the right and starts angling down. Follow along, ignoring the doors in the corner.

Stop about halfway down the sloping hall. Two doors, with a guard posted in front of each, are on either side of the hall. If you're low on ammo, set the Dragon for Proximity Mine and toss it between them. Otherwise, snipe them.

WARNING! You don't want to alert them until the Dragon is set, so don't get too close.

PERFECT DARK

Continue past the doors they were guarding and through the door at the end of the hall. It opens onto the hangar. The guards in there will shred you if you just charge in, so get their attention, then backpedal into the hall.

Get as high as you can up the hall while still being able to see the hangar door. As guards come through, cap them.

TIPS Using the Tranquilizer you picked up from the technicians helps you save ammo. You'll need rounds for your Dragon to complete the second objective.

Once the area is secure, cross the hangar floor and go up the ramp opposite the door. At the top, head to your left down the catwalk.

Pass through three doors and then examine the wall to your right. Down low is an opening. Crouch and poke your head through without falling off.

Check the area below for guards. Shoot if you need to. Drop down when it's safe and head to the left of the stack of boxes.

TIPS If you have more than one round for the Psychosis Gun, use one to tag a guard in here to help you clear the area.

Either shoot or Disarm the guards as they come around the stack, then head for the lift. You may need to hunt them down, but try to wait them out first. Letting them come to you increases your chances of survival.

Ride the lift up and run down the catwalk to the right as you exit the lift. Guards may run in from the other direction on the catwalk. Deal with them here or they'll dog your steps later on.

Through the door you'll see a guard with his back to you. Use the Psychosis Gun on him to mix things up. Sidestep to the right just after you shoot.

2 Once safely in this corner, use the Dragon to zoom in on the Maian saucer and destroy it. You'll burn through a clip and a half of ammo to send it up in a ball of fire. Or you can use your single Golden Magnum shot. Barring that, push the oil barrels closer to the saucer and blow them up to save ammo.

Follow the catwalk and take the right fork. Follow that to the elevator. A guard waits next to it, so blast him with the Dragon.

Between your Psychotic guard and the saucer explosion, the guards on this floor should be hurting. If your health is low, immediately go up the ramp next to the door you entered through. If you're healthy, wipe out the other guards with Dragon fire, collect ammo, and then go up the ramp.

SPECIAL ASSIGNMENTS

walkthrough

MIPS You're almost to the final objective, so use that ammo you've been saving.

Call the elevator and ride it to the top. There will be opponents either in the elevator when it shows up, or facing the elevator doors when it stops. Be prepared for either contingency.

Head left through the large door and take out the technician, if he's there, in the short hall. Then pass through the next large door.

To your right are a couple of guards who put up a futile effort to stop you. Put them down and go through the large door they guarded.

Pass through the second door into a large control room. More resistance awaits you here in the form of technicians. If you made a lot of noise earlier, they may have already come after you.

See that long row of partitions blocking the other half of the room? Blast one of them out of the way and go through. Once again, technicians will be waiting for you—unless they've already come after you.

1 After clearing the area, face the terminal in the center of the wall. Press ⑧ until you hear the keyboard. That clears your final objective.

You don't get much of a reward for your efforts, but the Carrington Institute has gotten the distress call.

Co-Operative Notes

Perhaps the most difficult of the Special Missions, Maian SOS is one where you'll need all the help you can get. The strategies are very similar, however, because ammo is still in short supply. Make sure both players are well equipped or else one will carry the whole team. Go after the guard with the gold Magnums and turn him with the Psychosis Gun. Take it slowly and cover each other as you work your way through the map and you'll do fine.

PERFECT DARK

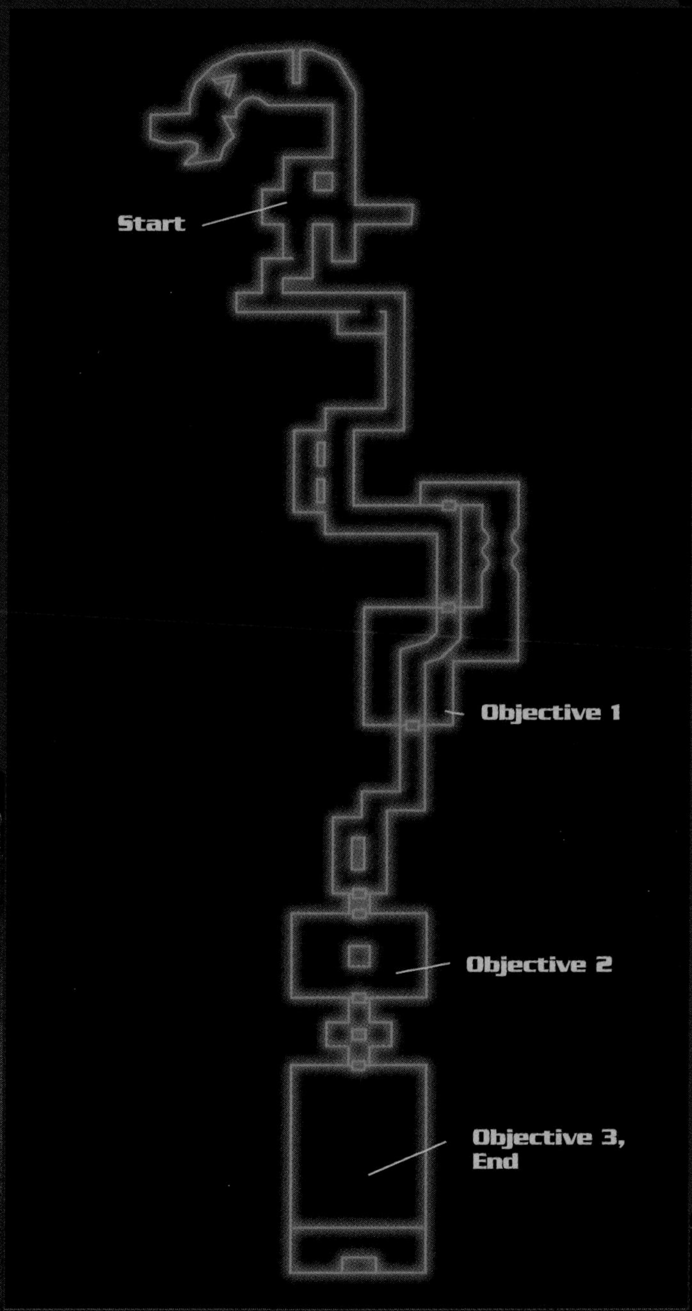

Start

War!

Background

The fleet bombardment has now ceased. Teams of Maian Protectors are being assembled for mopping up operations on the surface. Gene-spectrum scanning has brought another candidate for the Skedar King to our attention.

OBJECTIVES

★ ★ ★ 1. Kill Skedar King 1
★ ★ 2. Kill Skedar King 2
★ 3. Kill Skedar King 3

Look for the numbers in the red-bordered screenshots in the walkthrough.
They indicate which objective is being accomplished.

★ AGENT ★ SPECIAL AGENT ★ PERFECT AGENT

Objective 1

Objective 2

Objective 3,
End

NOTE

In War! the Skedar are numerous and send wave after wave of attackers to grind you down. You have two advantages. One, you have allies. Several Maian Protectors fight alongside you. They die often, but reinforcements will arrive. Two, you have a Phoenix. The explosive shells are your most effective tool against the Skedar.

As soon as the game starts, your Maian friends charge into the fray. Let them. Follow behind and they'll show you the way. (Actually, you can't get lost in this map, it's very straightforward.)

The other Maians don't have a very good survival instinct. They go toe-to-toe with the Skedars and usually lose. Support them by firing a few explosive shells at distant enemies.

Be careful about firing, though. Your allies are prone to step in front of your gun. This is not healthy for them or you.

This is the first really dangerous choke point. Your allies will most likely get wasted here. Go up the ramp and snipe down at the doors as the Skedar come through.

SPECIAL ASSIGNMENTS

walkthrough

TIPS

Don't stop moving. Standing still on the ramp and just firing will be the death of your Maian. Strafe as you shoot. Also, a cheap tactic is to simply stay on the ramp and snipe Skedar for as long as they come at you—which is a long time. This makes the later parts easier because there will be fewer enemies to face.

TIPS

Raising your sights before facing off with the Kings can help tremendously. It leaves you free to move about and fire without having to worry about aiming.

Watch out for Skedar on the bridge in this first "throne room." Don't turn the corner near the rotating column until there is a break in the Skedar onslaught: you don't want to deal with a horde of the beasts and a Skedar King at the same time.

1 Raise your gun sights and round the corner. You confront the first Skedar King. It uses a Reaper, so use the rotating column for cover if you need to. Go for headshots with the explosive Phoenix rounds and the King will drop. Your first objective is clear.

Go back to the ramp and up it. The door at the top is now unlocked. Blast any Skedar in your way and go through.

The bridge above the rotating column is another good place to play the waiting game with your Skedar foes. Pop them as they come through the door.

It's a good idea, even if you don't camp at the bridge, to wait for reinforcements before moving on. The extra firepower helps you get to the second King.

This room is just before the second King's room. Again, if you can, wait for reinforcements before tackling the King.

Move forward carefully, keeping the column directly in front of you. Slide to the side and you see the second King.

This monarch clone carries a Slayer Rocket Launcher. If you stay behind the column, you can fire a quick five shots into the King and put it down for good. With luck, the Skedar King won't even notice you. Grab the Slayer and carry on.

TIPS

If the King does notice you and charges, run away! It fires rockets as it comes after you. Luckily, the King manages to hurt itself with the explosions from time to time.

2

The Skedar just keep coming. Stand by the column and blast the Skedar that come through the door. Wait for reinforcements if you can. As soon as the stream of enemies slacks off, run into the room.

There may still be plenty of Skedar that want to stop you, so stay sharp. Run around the block in the middle of the room, equip the Slayer, and go through the next door.

This is the main throne room, home of your final foe. Fire the Slayer at the Skedar King as soon as you enter. Then strafe to the side.

2 If you don't hit the King the first time, circle around the room, keeping your back to the wall and the King in your sights. Fire the Slayer, but keep moving. One rocket hit puts an end to the Skedar King's life and your mission.

It's time to celebrate.

Co-Operative Notes

War! is a straight shot from beginning to end, but the Skedar's sheer weight of numbers makes it difficult. You can use the extra help from a buddy to even the odds. Cover each other as you move through the Ruins and concentrate fire on single enemies to drop them faster. This helps clear out resistance faster. The key is to not get too far ahead of each other. There's safety in numbers.

The Duel

Background

Final Test. Defeat the holographic simulated opponent.

Carrington//I have every confidence in your abilities, Joanna. Pay attention to the test, and use all of the experience you picked up throughout your training. Good luck.

OBJECTIVES

★ ★ ★ 1. Defeat dataDyne guard

★ ★ 2. Defeat Jonathan Dark

★ 3. Defeat Trent Easton

Look for the numbers in the red-bordered screenshots in the walkthrough. They indicate which objective is being accomplished.

★ AGENT ★ **SPECIAL AGENT** ★ PERFECT AGENT

A classic duel. Take a few steps, turn, and fire.

You'll automatically take the steps forward, so keep the control stick pressed to the left or right (whichever you prefer). As soon as you regain control, Joanna swings around to face the dataDyne guard.

SPECIAL ASSIGNMENTS

The guard sidesteps quickly, straightens up, then shoots. If you don't move the guard will hit you with his first shot. So, either run or fire back.

Being quick on the draw is what duels are usually about, but you're a covert agent, so being sneaky is all right. To test your accuracy under pressure, simply attempt to line up a headshot before you get capped.

If you decide to run, head to Joanna's right as soon as you regain control and duck around the partition.

1 Quickly run to the other end, strafe out, and fire on the confused guard. Pick up the Falcon he drops if you need the ammo.

TIPS If you don't come around the partition quickly, the guard catches on to what you're doing and will be ready for it.

Once you've taken care of the dataDyne guard you must go against Jonathan Dark.

Take the steps, turn around, and...where'd he go?

Jonathan knows all about sneaky tricks. He's behind the partition. Lower your aim and wait for him to come rolling out. Fire at will.

2 Jonathan's stealthy, but his aim is awful. You can stand still for a few shots, but don't press your luck. When he's toast, Jonathan drops a Magnum for you to take if you need it.

Next up is Trent Easton. This guy is a perfect shot. Give him a second to aim and you're dead.

Try Jonathan's tactic against Trent. Run. Go around the partition as fast as you can and pop out. You have to be dead-on accurate. One shot is all you'll get before Trent shoots you.

3 Get off a good shot and you'll defeat the third opponent.

PERFECT DARK™

Perfect Dark **contains a large amount of gameplay in the Single Player section alone. But it's in the Combat Simulator that you'll find an almost infinite amount of games and challenges to keep you coming back.**

We'll describe your menu options first and then go into Scenarios, where the rules of engagement are set. Finally, you'll find a section devoted to maps of all the multiplayer Arenas.

Menus

The Combat Simulator is full of choices. You can control almost all aspects of the game, even down to the personalities of the Simulants you face.

From the Perfect menu choose "Combat Simulator". You'll be given four choices:

* **CHALLENGES: See the "Challenges" section of this guide for details.**

* **LOAD/PRESET GAMES: Allows you to load saved games or choose from a list of presets, games with interesting twists in the rules.**

* **QUICK START: Gets you into a multiplayer Scenario quickly. You can change several options.**

* **ADVANCED SETUP: Allows you the most choice in setting up a game. It has all the choices of Quick Start and more.**

The Combat Simulator menu. Choices, choices…

Challenges have their own section in this guide and Load/Preset Games are self-explanatory. So, we'll jump straight to the Quick Start option.

Quick Start

The unique part of the Quick Start is the Quick Team menu. It gives you all the combinations of Players and Simulants you need. Using it eliminates the need to manually set who's on what team.

Here you'll find all the arrangements you can make of Player and Simulant. The type of game you want to play determines the choice you make.

Once you've chosen from the Quick Team menu, you're sent to a second options menu. The "Simulant Difficulty" selection is worth mentioning here. You can't choose Special Simulant Types, only Normal ones.

The other settings are repeated in the Advanced Setup, so we'll check that out now.

Advanced Setup

This is the mother lode. From here you can control the details of the games you play. We'll give you a rundown of what everything in this section does. You can use the Control Stick to move through four different menus:

GAME SETUP

PLAYER SETUP

STUFF

COMBAT CHALLENGES

Combat Challenges is so large that it has its own section in this strategy guide. Check it out for more information on the Challenges.

Now we'll take a look at the other menus.

GAME SETUP//Most decisions are made here, from location of the battle to how many players will participate.

The Game Setup menu

Scenario//See the "Scenario" section below for descriptions of the different games and strategies for each.

Options//Several of the parameters you can set with Options are common for Scenarios.

OPTION	EFFECT
One-Hit Kills	One shot from any weapon will kill your target.
Slow Motion	Slows down the action. (Smart Slow Motion only slows down encounters with opponents.)
Fast Movement	Increases game speed
Display Team	When playing with more than one human player, a colored line indicates which team you're on.
No Radar	Toggles your radar on or off
No Auto-Aim	Toggles auto-aim on or off
Kills Score	Allows points for kills in non-Combat Scenarios

Scenario-Specific Options

Option	Scenario Where Used	Effect
NO PLAYER HIGHLIGHT	COMBAT	Without highlight, players are harder to see
NO PICKUP HIGHLIGHT	COMBAT	With highlight, pickups flash
HIGHLIGHT BRIEFCASE	HOLD THE BRIEFCASE	Briefcase is bright
SHOW ON RADAR	HOLD THE BRIEFCASE	Briefcase is a green box on radar
HIGHLIGHT TERMINAL	HACKER CENTRAL	Terminal and Data Uplink glow
SHOW ON RADAR	HACKER CENTRAL	Terminal and Data Uplink are green boxes on radar
HIGHLIGHT TARGET	POP A CAP	Target player glows green
SHOW ON RADAR	POP A CAP	Target player is an open circle on radar
HILL ON RADAR	KING OF THE HILL	Location of hill is an open box on radar
MOBILE HILL	KING OF THE HILL	Once hill is captured it moves location
TIME	KING OF THE HILL	Adjusts how long a team must hold the hill to earn points
SHOW ON RADAR	CAPTURE THE CASE	Team bases and players holding briefcases are shown on radar

Arena//
Here you can choose which multiplayer map you'll play on. A section below details each of the Arenas and their layouts.

Weapons//
With this option you can set the weapons and devices that appear in your game. You can make a custom set or choose one of the Weapons Sets offered.

Pistols:	Automatics:	Power:	FarSight:	Tranquilizer:	Heavy:
Falcon 2	Falcon 2	MagSec 4	Phoenix	Falcon 2	Mauler
MagSec 4	CMP150	DY357	Cyclone	CMP150	K7 Avenger
Phoenix	Laptop Gun	Shotgun	Callisto NTG	Dragon	Reaper
Mauler	AR34	RC-P120	FarSight XR-20	Tranquilizer	SuperDragon
Shield	Shield	Shield	Shield	Shield	Shield

Golden Magnum:	Explosive:	Grenade Launcher:	Rocket Launcher:	Proximity Mine:	Close Combat:
Falcon 2 (silencer)	Devastator	MagSec 4	Mauler	MagSec 4	Combat Knife
Grenade	Devastator	CMP150	Cyclone	Laptop Gun	Combat Knife
CMP150	SuperDragon	AR34	Dragon	K7 Avenger	Timed Mine
DY357-LX	SuperDragon	Devastator	Rocket Launcher	Proximity Mine	Crossbow
Shield	Shield	Shield	Shield	Shield	Shield

Random Five is just what it sounds like: five random weapon types. Random selects six weapon types at random. Custom is for you to play with.

When customizing the Weapons Set you should understand the selections "Nothing" and "Disabled."

Selecting Nothing for a slot just means that no weapons will appear in that slot. Places where you would normally find a weapon will be empty. Disabling a slot means that those pickup areas will be filled with another slot's weapon.

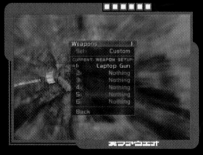

With a Laptop Gun in slot 1 and Nothing selected for the rest, there will be very, very few weapons.

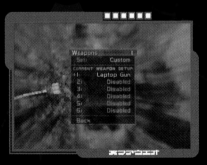

With a Laptop Gun in slot 1 and Disable selected for the rest, you'll find a *ton* of Laptop Guns and *nothing but* Laptop Guns.

PERFECT DARK™

Limits//
In this section you can set what conditions must be met to end the game. You can select how much time you'll be able to play, from 1 to 60 minutes or unlimited. A score limit can be set as well, from 1 to 100 points or unlimited. If you're playing teams, you can set the Team Score from 1 to 400 or unlimited.

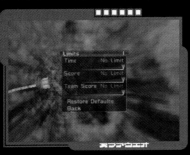
If you don't set any limits, the game will never end.

Player Handicaps//
Here you can increase or decrease the health of a player to even the playing field. Perhaps you want to give your friend—who has never played *Perfect Dark* before—a bit of an edge so you won't get bored running all over him. Bump his Handicap up or yours down. You can set health at anywhere from 10 to 1,000 percent—100 percent is normal.

With a 1,000 percent Handicap, this player will be hard to beat.

Simulants//
This is where you can load Simulants to compete against you. Check out the "Simulants" section of this guide for an in-depth explanation of this option.

Teams//
Under Team Control you can set up teams of players for co-operative multiplayer games. Auto Team lets you quick pick teams: Humans vs. Simulants, Two or Three Teams, etc.

Load Settings/Save Settings//
Under this option you can load up the preset games' previously saved settings that you put together yourself. Save Settings is where you save game setups that you want to remember—perhaps your favorite Custom Weapons Set or a good mix of Simulants.

This menu lets you play with your friends or against them.

PLAYER SETUP//
This menu allows you to customize your character. Take the time to create your standard character and always use it in the multiplayer games. Your statistics will build up, raising you in rank.

Character//
This is where you create the look of your alter ego. Move the Control Stick up to get to the Faces menu and down to get to the Body menu. Push the Control Stick left and right to scroll through your choices.

NOTE

The more Challenges you open, the more choices you'll have for bodies and faces.

You can look as good as you feel.

Control//The Control options are numerous. Fiddle with them to figure out your preferences. Generally, the default controls are handy.

The standard menu for Control.

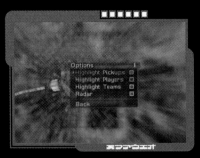

Bright, flashing pickups help, especially if you're a beginning player or don't know the multiplayer maps well.

Player Options//For Player Options we have one suggestion: turn on Highlight Pickups. It makes ammo and weapons much easier to see as you run through the levels. This comes in handy in the Challenges, where you need any edge you can get.

Statistics//Your statistics accrue over every game you play, win or lose. Tallies of the Medals you have won, distance your character has run, accuracy, shots fired, etc. are all recorded and displayed. As they build up, your title will change. It takes a lot to reach the top. You need to increase all your stats. The title doesn't gain you anything in the game, but it shows how dedicated you are to *Perfect Dark*.

You can earn Medals in multiplayer games and Challenges. They act as an incentive to work on your accuracy and survival instincts. Keep trying to earn Medals as you play—the practice hones your skills for the harder Challenges and human players you'll face.

You can earn four Medals: Accuracy, Head Shot, Kill Master, and Survivor.

Another human player must be in the game to earn Medals in Accuracy and Head Shot.

STUFF//The Stuff menu holds a random assortment of options for the multi-player games.

The Soundtrack option is straightforward. You can pick the music from a selection of tracks from the game.

Team Names is another basic option. If you're tired of simply being called "The Red Team" you can type in your own handle.

Lock is interesting. This option allows you to choose who gets to decide on the next game. For example, if you choose Last Loser, then the person who comes in last sets the parameters for the next game.

Lock can keep one player from dominating.

multiplayer

Ratio helps keep the game within your screen. If anything's being cut off by the edges of your TV, try changing the Ratio.

Split gives you the choice of how the screen looks in a two-player game. Vertical gives you more view up and down and less to the left and right. Horizontal gives better vision to the sides.

We prefer the Horizontal view because it gives better peripheral vision. This helps you see players coming up on you (or lets you see who just shot you).

Vertical

Horizontal

> **NOTE**
> For information on the Combat Challenges, see the "Challenges" section of this guide.

Scenarios

Now that the details are out of the way, let's get to the games themselves. You can choose from six preset Scenarios. Each has a unique twist that requires specific strategies to handle.

Combat

The most basic of all multiplayer games, Combat is a simple match of skill and marksmanship. You run through the map, searching out opponents and weapons. Pick up the weapons you find and use them against the opponents you find.

You can use teams in Combat Scenarios. The team with the most kills wins.

To win at Combat games, you'll need to work on several aspects of your gameplay. First, train to bring your accuracy up. Winning and losing can hinge on hitting your enemy first—specially against the higher Difficulty Simulants.

A classic Combat moment: everyone's accounted for.

Because you can't play effectively if you don't have the right tools, knowing where to find weapons and items is important. In general, you need a good knowledge of the whole map. Specifically, you need to know where each and every item spawns.

That's what you want to see: your enemy's head lined up in your sights.

Knowing the location of a Shield can increase your chances of survival.

> **TIPS**
> It's always a good idea to start playing with Highlight Pickups checked in the Player Setup. This helps familiarize you with the item locations.

TIPS Knowing the maps is essential to success in every multiplayer game. Spend some time running around on them by yourself to get a feel for them.

Finally, make sure you know how to move. If you've gone through the holo training and/or the single-player game, you're already familiar with the controls. However, in multiplayer games the movement can be much more frantic. Your enemies are constantly moving, and the high level Simulants are better than you are at moving and firing. So practice firing while pelting around a level, running backward, falling, etc.

Four humans can be a messy but fun game.

With all that in mind, practice, practice, practice. Experience counts for a lot in the multiplayer games. Remember, though, that even the best of the Simulants aren't as unpredictable as human opponents. The PerfectSims and DarkSims still have patterns that they will never break, but your friends will learn and adapt. Good luck.

Hold the Briefcase

A briefcase is loose in this game and your job is to find and hold onto it. Of course, everyone else wants it too.

When the case isn't held by any player, it shows up as a green circle on the radar. Run for it. When a player has the briefcase, he'll glow green and show up as a circle on the radar.

When you're holding the case, a timer starts counting down at the top of the screen. When it hits zero you get a point.

When someone else has the case, hunt him down. As soon as you blast him, he'll drop the case. Snap it up and head for cover.

Depending on the number of other players, you may want to find a safe place to hole up when you have the briefcase. Get your back to a wall and find a place where you can see all approaches. Nail your opponents as they come up on you.

Now you wait. Keep an eye on the radar to watch your opponents.

There's the briefcase, just lying there. What are you waiting for? Grab it!

This is a great spot in the G5 Building Arena—especially with a Laptop Gun—but don't make it a habit.

With four of you against four of them, keep up the chatter so you can actually work as a team.

This is a safe and sane way to rack up points, but might cause some of your friends to complain. Save this tactic (called "camping") for the Challenges. Simulants don't care if you do it.

You can enable teams in Hold the Briefcase, which changes things considerably. When you have allies, you can cover each other or flank the briefcase carrier. Keep talking to your teammates. There's no point in having teams if you don't work together.

multiplayer

Hacker Central

This Scenario has a simple premise: Find the Data Uplink and use it to download information from the Terminal (which you must also find).

When you first play, make sure the Uplink and Terminal are highlighted on the radar. The first few minutes of each of these games will be a mad scramble for the Data Uplink.

If you grab it, head to the Terminal—which is the other green circle on the radar. Once there, select the Data Uplink from your inventory, aim it at the Terminal, and press the trigger. You'll begin downloading.

This guy has ahold of the briefcase. You know what to do.

While you're using the Data Uplink you're very vulnerable. You can't move far from the Terminal and you can't switch to a weapon or the connection will be broken.

NOTE The Data Uplink is small and hard to see. If you can't find it where the radar says it should be, scour the area before checking different floors.

After a few moments, the download will be complete and you'll score. If you aren't being shot at, press the trigger again to start another download.

If you don't grab the Uplink first, run for the Terminal. The player with the Uplink has to show up or he won't score. Stake out the spot and pop him when he gets there.

Once the player carrying the Data Uplink is taken out, the Uplink reappears in a different location. However, if you're right next to a player who gets shot down, you may get lucky and snatch the Uplink out of the air as it drops.

Whack him quickly or he'll finish the download.

Because you're virtually defenseless while downloading, it's a hairy business to go up against two or more opponents when you're alone. It's best to enable teams and have one player download while the other guards.

Catch!

Take along a friend to guard your back.

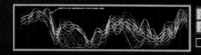

Pop a Cap

This Scenario is a fun one. It can be a long game if you turn off the Kills Score option—which we recommend. The cap cycles through all players and Sims in the same order.

It works like this: A player is chosen at random as the "Victim." Whoever it is shows up as a circle on the radar and glows green.

Without the Kills Score option, the only way to score is to cap the Victim—two points—or stay alive when you are the Victim—one point for every minute.

This player is "It." Pop a cap in him.

You score more for getting the Victim, but every time a Victim is killed, another player is randomly chosen to be "It."

Hunting down the Victim is straightforward. Follow the radar. (If you turn off the radar it's easier for the Victims to survive.)

Ever feel like everyone's out to get you?

As the Victim, your job is a bit harder. You have to fend off everyone else. The Laptop Gun's Sentry Gun mode can help immensely; it's the only friend you'll have.

With teams enabled, Pop a Cap becomes similar to Hold the Briefcase. Therefore, we don't recommend teams for this Scenario. Pop a Cap is more fun as a free-for-all.

King of the Hill

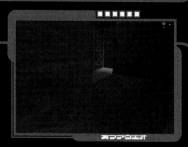

This Scenario is a classic game translated into the *Perfect Dark* world. The object is to get to the "hill"—a specific area in the Arena—and guard it against the other team. Or, if your opponents already have possession of the hill, get there and take it away from them.

Once a team gets control of the hill, it changes to that team's color in the game and on the radar. A timer starts—the default is 20 seconds. If the team holds onto the hill for that long, they score a point.

The green area is the hill. It's green until a team takes possession of it.

There must be a member of the team in the hill for all 30 seconds. If the Red Team has the hill and then everyone steps out of the colored area, the hill reverts to green and the timer resets.

Also, if there are any members of the opposing team in the boundaries of the hill, the timer stops counting down. You'll need to clear the area before the timer will start again.

Camping isn't a bad thing in King of the Hill. It's the whole point. Here, all entrances are covered.

This enemy is trying to muscle in on your turf. Don't let him.

If the other team grabs hold of the hill, have at least one of your team rush in with guns blazing. You may chase them out of the hill, kill them all, or simply stop the clock for a while.

As with all the multiplayer games, knowing the maps helps immensely. Being able to quickly find the hill increases your chances of scoring.

8 6 6 5 5 6 6 5 6 6 6 5   2 1 0   2   0 0 1 2   2 1 0 0 0 0 0 1

PERFECT DARK ™

NOTE

You can set the options so that the hill is in the same place during the entire game. The Mobile Hill option, though, makes for a more interesting time because there are a few frantic moments while teams rush to the next hill.

Capture the Case

Another classic game, this Scenario is based on Capture the Flag. Both teams have a base with a briefcase inside. The object is to infiltrate the enemy's base, pick up their briefcase, and make it back to your base. Meanwhile, the opposing team will be attempting the same thing.

This Scenario is best played with teams. Detail some players to guard your base while the others go after your opponent's case. Realize that they're going to do the same thing, so if you're storming the enemy base, expect serious resistance.

If someone snaps up your briefcase, chase him down. As soon as a carrier falls, the briefcase is returned to the base.

Also, if you have the case, you have to run over your own case to score. When your case is missing, you can't gain any points. When you have the enemy briefcase but yours is missing, send another player to track down the enemy carrier. Don't risk getting killed and losing the enemy briefcase by tracking him down yourself.

This is your briefcase. Defend it with your life—or your teammate's.

Your opponents won't just give up their case. You have to take it. Two players guard their case carrier while the fourth player hunts for the enemy carrier.

Arena Maps

This section includes all the multiplayer Arena maps. The circled letters (Ⓐ) show where the different floors connect. They indicate stairs, ramps, elevators, even holes in the ground. Each map also shows where items and weapons spawn (🛡). Where a specific weapon—such as a Falcon 2—appears depends on which slot it occupies in the Weapons Set. Study the item spots so you can find the tools you need in a hurry.

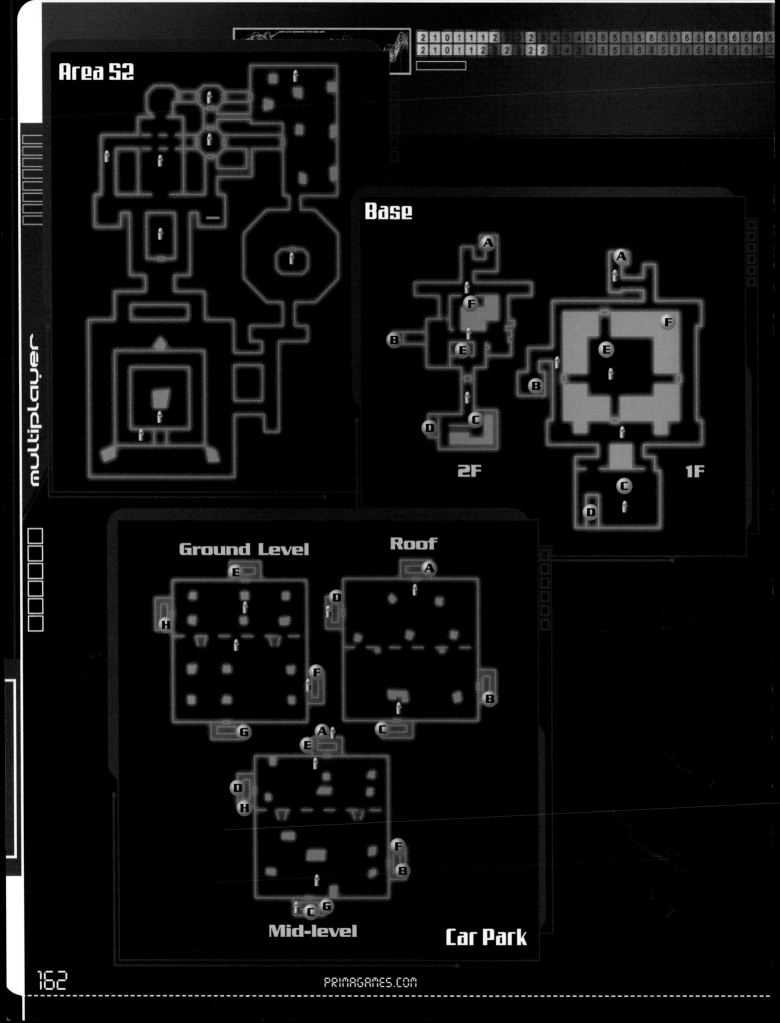

Area 52

Base

A

A

F

B

E

F

B

E

B

C

D

C

2F

D

1F

C

D

Ground Level

Roof

E

A

H

D

F

B

G

C

A

E

D

H

F

B

C

G

Mid-level

Car Park

Complex

Sub 1

1F

H

E

C

B

D

A

E

C

B

A

H

D

F

2F

F

G

2F

G

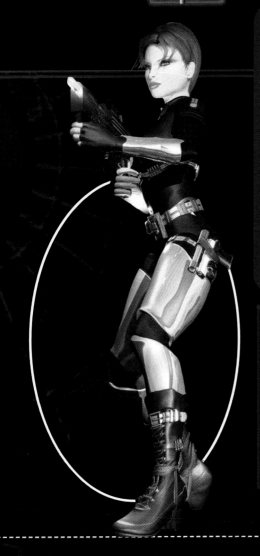

Felicity

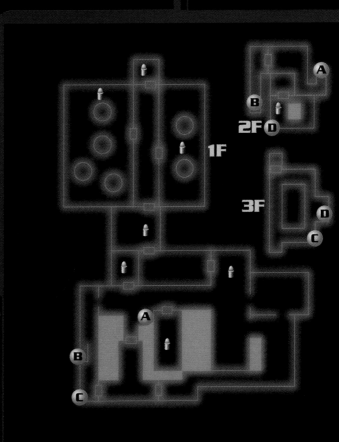

A

B

D

2F

3F

D

C

1F

A

B

C

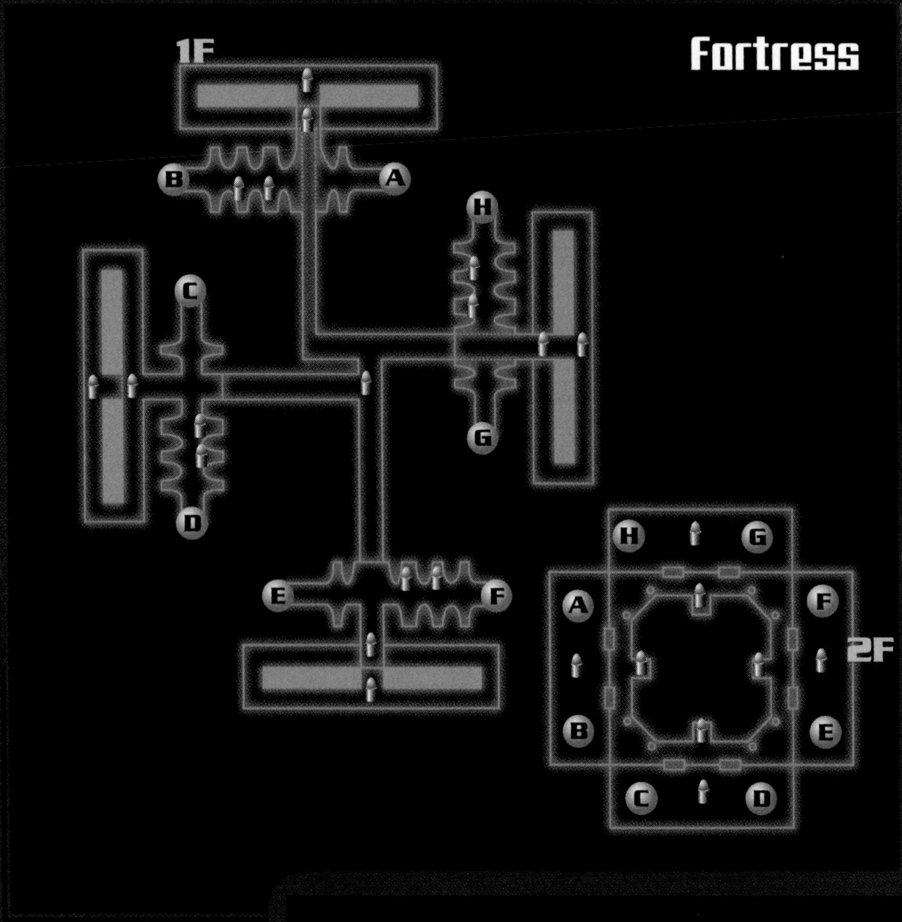

1F

Fortress

B A

H

C

G

D

E F

2F

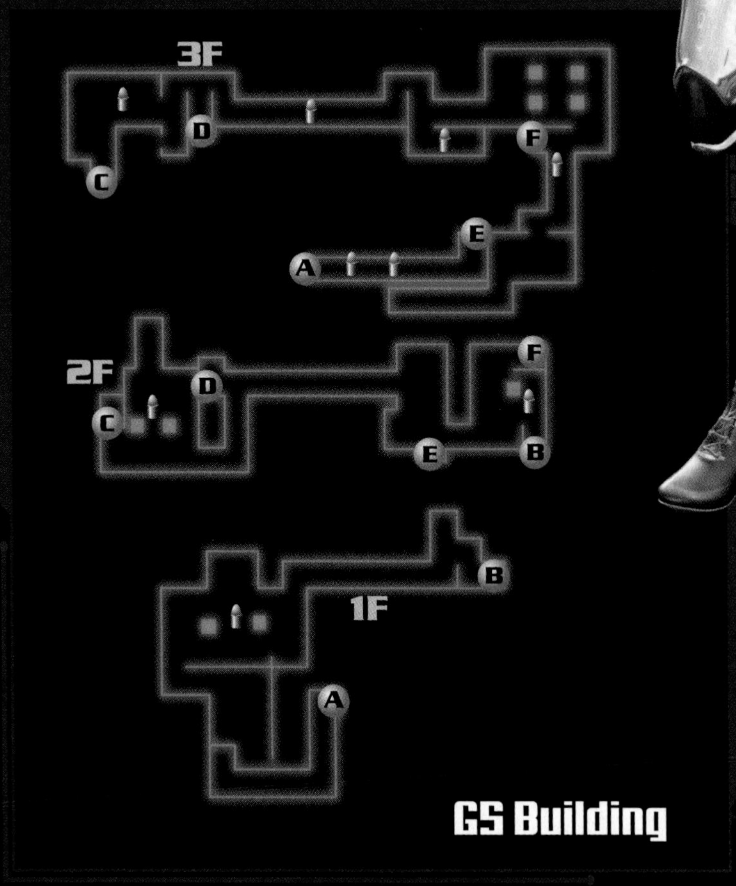

H G

A F

B E

C D

3F

C D F

E

A

2F

C D F

E B

1F

B

A

GS Building

PERFECT DARK™

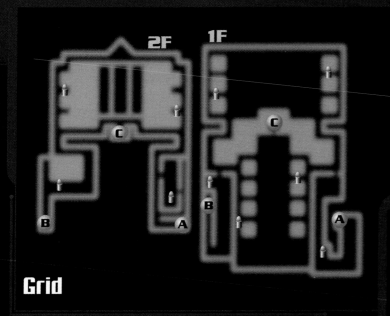

Grid

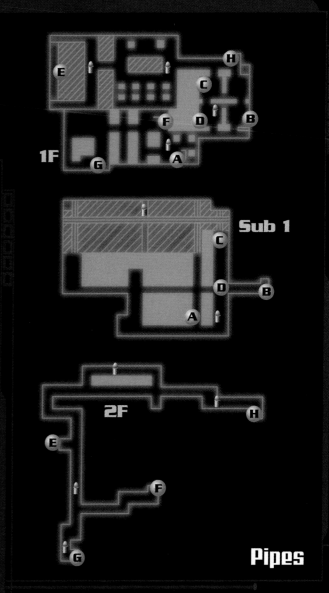

1F

Sub 1

2F

Pipes

3F

2F

2F

3F

4F

5F

1F

Ravine

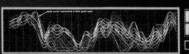

Ruins

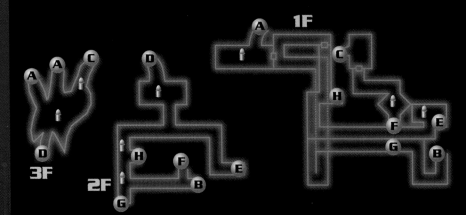

1F

3F

2F

Mid Levels

Top Levels

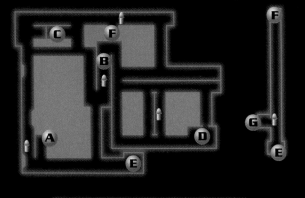

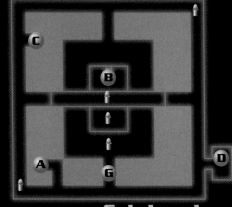

Sub Levels

Sewers

Skedar

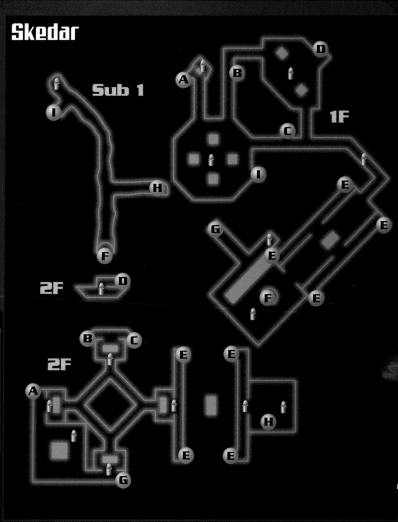

Sub 1

I

A
B
D
C
1F
I
H
E
E
G
E
E
F
F
E

2F
D
F

2F
B C
A
E E
H
E E
G

Temple

2F

D
D
1F
A B
B A
C C
C

Villa

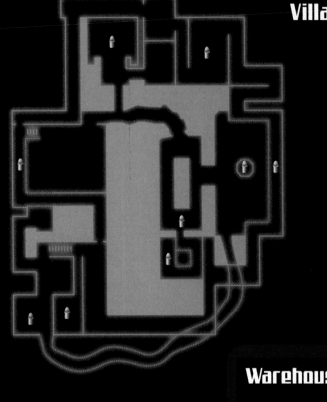

Warehouse

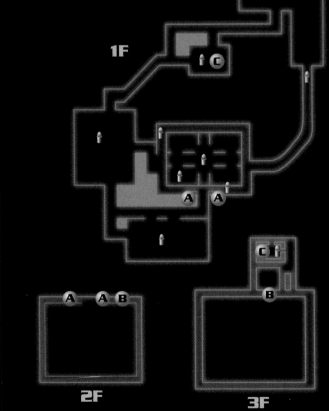

1F

2F

3F

The Cheats Table

This table lists all the cheats that you can unlock with various feats of gameplay. Some of them are self-explanatory or become obvious when you enable them. Others aren't so clear.

Below the table you'll find explanations of the difficult cheats.

Cheat	Mission	Difficulty	Time to Complete Level
FUN	—	—	—
DK Mode	Chicago—Stealth	Any	Complete
Play as Elvis	Area 51—Rescue	Perfect Agent	7:59
Slo-Mo Single Player	dataDyne Research—Investigation	Any	Complete
Small Characters	Area 51—Infiltration	Any	Complete
Small Jo	G5 Building—Reconnaissance	Any	Complete
Team Heads Only	Air Base—Espionage	Any	Complete
GAMEPLAY	—	—	—
Cloaking Device	G5 Building—Reconnaissance	Agent	1:40
Every Enemy Has Rocket Launcher	*Pelagic II*—Exploration	Any	Complete
Every Enemy Shielded	Carrington Institute—Defense	Any	Complete
Invincible	Area 51—Escape	Agent	3:50
Jo Shield	Deep Sea—Nullify Threat	Any	—
Marquis of Queensbury Rules	dataDyne Central—Defection	Special Agent	1:30
Perfect Darkness	Crash Site—Confrontation	Any	Complete
Super Shield	Carrington Institute—Defense	Agent	1:45

secrets and bonuses

Cheat	Mission	Difficulty	Time to Complete Level
WEAPONS FOR JO IN SOLO	—	—	—
FarSight	Deep Sea—Nullify Threat	Perfect Agent	7:27
Laptop Gun	*Air Force One*—Antiterrorism	Any	Complete
Phoenix	Attack Ship—Covert Assault	Any	Complete
Psychosis Gun	Chicago—Stealth	Perfect Agent	2:00
Rocket Launcher	dataDyne Central—Extraction	Any	Complete
Sniper Rifle	Carrington Villa—Hostage One	Any	Complete
SuperDragon	Area 51—Escape	Any	Complete
Trent's Magnum	Crash Site—Confrontation	Agent	2:50
CLASSIC WEAPONS FOR JO IN SOLO	—	—	—
AR53	Carrington Institute Firing Range	Gold	Complete
CC13	Carrington Institute Firing Range	Gold	Complete
DMC	Carrington Institute Firing Range	Gold	Complete
KF7 Special	Carrington Institute Firing Range	Gold	Complete
KLO1313	Carrington Institute Firing Range	Gold	Complete
PP9I	Carrington Institute Firing Range	Gold	Complete
RC-P45	Carrington Institute Firing Range	Gold	Complete
ZZT (9mm)	Carrington Institute Firing Range	Gold	Complete
WEAPONS	—	—	—
All Guns in Solo	Skedar Ruins—Battle Shrine	Perfect Agent	5:31
Classic Sight	dataDyne Central—Defection	Any	Complete
Hurricane Fists	dataDyne Central—Extraction	Agent	2:03
R-Tracker/Weapon Cache Location	Skedar Ruins—Battle Shrine	Any	Complete
Unlimited Ammo	*Pelagic II*—Exploration	Special Agent	7:07
Unlimited Ammo—Laptop Gun	*Air Force One*—Antiterrorism	Perfect Agent	3:55
Unlimited Ammo, No Reloads	Air Base—Espionage	Special Agent	3:11
X-Ray Scanner	Area 51—Rescue	Any	Complete

The Cheats Table CONTINUED

Cheat	Mission	Difficulty	Time to Complete Level
BUDDIES	—	—	—
Alien	Attack Ship—Covert Assault	Special Agent	5:17
Hit and Run	Carrington Villa— Hostage One	Special Agent	2:30
Hotshot	Area 51—Infiltration	Special Agent	5:00
Pugilist	dataDyne Research— Investigation	Perfect Agent	6:30
Velvet Dark	N/A	Available by Default	N/A

a few notes on the cheats table

MARQUIS OF QUEENSBURY RULES//If you're a sporting chap you may want to try the Marquis of Queensbury Rules Cheat. Enemies then attack using classic boxing styles. A single tap on the chin puts them down for the count. Of course, nothing prevents you from using weapons.

The Marquis of Queensbury Rules do not apply to multiplayer games. FistSims fit the bill if you want boxing in multiplayer.

PERFECT DARKNESS//Lights out! This cheat removes all the electric lighting from the levels—you can still see the moon. Fortunately, you'll be equipped with Night Vision equipment to aid your missions. The darkness helps you sneak up on enemies, but don't get too close.

CLASSIC WEAPONS FOR JO IN SOLO//At the Firing Range you can earn medals for training performance. Getting the gold unlocks several classic weapons for use. Earn the gold with every weapon except the Laser to get all that's available.

R-TRACKER/WEAPON CACHE LOCATION//Enable the radar and it will show you where the secret weapon caches are. (The walkthrough also points them out.)

Game Boy Cheats

If you have *Perfect Dark* for the Game Boy and the N64, and a Transfer Pak, you can get four of the cheats immediately on the N64 version.

Load the Game Boy cartridge into the Transfer Pak and turn on your N64. Make sure you start a level on the N64 version before you power down. This gives you the following cheats:

All Guns in Solo

Cloaking Device

Hurricane Fists

R-Tracker/Weapon Cache Location

Hidden Items

You can find a ton of Items in *Perfect Dark*. You have to meet certain conditions, but most result in more effective weapons for your use.

Mission	Item	Location
DATADYNE CENTRAL—DEFECTION	LAPTOP GUN IN PERFECT AGENT	Let the programmer run ahead of Joanna. He opens a locked door near the elevators.
DATADYNE CENTRAL—DEFECTION	DOUBLE FALCON 2	Dropped by the helmeted guard on the third floor down
DATADYNE RESEARCH—INVESTIGATION	DOUBLE CMP150	Get to the weapons locker control without being seen. The locker is near the maintenance bot.
DATADYNE RESEARCH—INVESTIGATION	PROXIMITY MINE	On the floor behind the isotope
DATADYNE CENTRAL—EXTRACTION	GRENADE, DRAGON	Take out the guards on the bottom floor without being seen. Eliminate the guard around the corner, at the top of the first elevator. He drops a key to Cassandra's office. A Grenade is on Cassandra's desk. Use the Grenade in the right corner of the office as you face the windows. The Dragon is through the hole.

Mission	Item	Location
DATADYNE CENTRAL—EXTRACTION	DY357 MAGNUM	Drop the first five guards without being seen. The fifth guard drops a Magnum.
CARRINGTON VILLA—HOSTAGE ONE	DEVASTATOR	Shoot the crate sitting by itself on the helipad. Find ammo for the Devastator by shooting crates.
CARRINGTON VILLA—HOSTAGE ONE	DOUBLE CMP150	Dropped by the sniper next to the helipad. Take him out in less than 38 seconds.
CARRINGTON VILLA—HOSTAGE ONE	SNIPER RIFLE IN PERFECT AGENT	In the bedroom
CHICAGO—STEALTH	BOMBSPY	Inside the trash bin next to the stacked barrels. Move the trash bin by a barrel, then blow up the barrel.

NOTE: Using the BombSpy on the guards at the mission exit allows the player to bypass reprogramming the taxi.

Mission	Item	Location
CHICAGO—STEALTH	DOUBLE FALCON 2 (SCOPE)	In the Pond Punk on the bar to the left of the entrance. The last door into the Pond Punk is usually locked. To gain access, make some noise while eliminating the guards outside. This draws the guards inside to come out. This may not work all the time.
G5 BUILDING—RECONNAISSANCE	CROSSBOW	Knock out the second guard in the first area with fists or pistol whip him.
G5 BUILDING—RECONNAISSANCE	N-BOMB	By the top exit, up the stairwell, above the safe. You must place the remote mine at the top of the stairwell in **Chicago—Stealth** (the previous mission). Chicago must be played in Special and Perfect Agent modes only.
AREA 51—INFILTRATION	DOUBLE MAGSEC 4	Take out the red-and-white guard standing by the satellite dish.

NOTE: In Special and Perfect Agent modes the guard appears after placing the Comms Rider bug.

Mission	Item	Location
AREA 51—RESCUE	DOUBLE FALCON 2 (SILENCER)	Destroy a barrel located on the bottom of a stack to the right of the first ramp.
AREA 51—RESCUE	PHOENIX	Remember the civilian by that first Robot Intercepter in Area 51—Infiltration? If you let him live when taking his key, you'll have access to a Phoenix on this level. Go to the door above the starting point. Shoot the door and that same civilian will open it from the other side. Take the elevator in this area to the top level. The Phoenix is on a bench by the windows in the hangar control room.

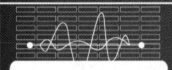

secrets and bonuses

Mission	Item	Location
AREA 51—ESCAPE	THREE REMOTE MINES	Get Elvis to the containment area in less than 36 seconds. The Remote Mines are just inside the first room with red-and-white guards.
AREA 51—ESCAPE	DOUBLE FALCON 2 (SCOPE)	On the ground near the two lab technicians at the start of the mission
AIR BASE—ESPIONAGE	DOUBLE DY357 MAGNUM	Dropped by the last of the three NSA guards after you knock them out.
AIR BASE—ESPIONAGE	FOUR PROXIMITY MINES	On the left side at the end of the path the flight attendant comes from.
AIR FORCE ONE—ANTITERRORISM	DOUBLE CYCLONE	Knock out the two Secret Service agents at the base of the stairs. Use their key cards to open the two closets.
CRASH SITE—CONFRONTATION	PROXIMITY MINE	Talk to Elvis by the UFO before completing any objectives.
CRASH SITE—CONFRONTATION	HOVERBIKE	Lower the HoverBike in the *Air Force One* cargo bay during the previous mission. The HoverBike will be next to the player at the start.
CRASH SITE—CONFRONTATION	DY357-LX	Disarm Trent
PELAGIC II—EXPLORATION	DOUBLE FALCON 2 (SILENCER)	Kill the guard after the fourth door from the start. You must go straight through the hall to that point without the alarm going off.
DEEP SEA—NULLIFY THREAT	THREE PROXIMITY MINES	Eliminate the guard to the far left after the fourth door. Joanna must get him before Elvis does.
CARRINGTON INSTITUTE—DEFENSE	DEVASTATOR	Rescue the two hostages in the Information Lab without any other hostages dying. They give Joanna the Devastator.
ATTACK SHIP—COVERT ASSAULT	DOUBLE MAULER	Dropped by the middle Skedar on the bridge
SKEDAR RUINS—BATTLE SHRINE	DOUBLE PHOENIX	Destroy the two remaining temple targets with the Devastator. The pistol appears at the edge of the ravine.
MR. BLONDE'S REVENGE	DOUBLE CMP150	Dropped by a guard in the room before the lab elevator
MAIAN S.O.S.	PSYCHOSIS GUN	Don't use it on technicians at the start. Push the hover bed to windows and blow them out. Use the Psychosis Gun on guard with the Double DY357-LX (in the round room with the back exit to the hangar).
MAIAN S.O.S.	DOUBLE DY357-LX	Dropped by the guard in the round room with the back exit to the hangar (see entry above).

PRIMA'S OFFICIAL STRATEGY GUIDE

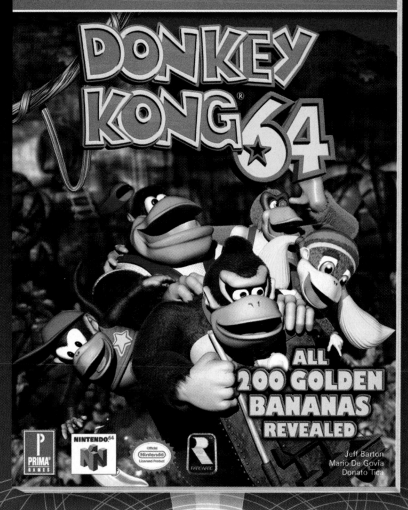

DONKEY KONG 64

ALL 200 GOLDEN BANANAS REVEALED

Jeff Barton
Mario De Govia
Donato Tica

WE'VE GOT STRATEGY COVERED

Prima GAMES

primagames.com

PRIMA'S OFFICIAL STRATEGY GUIDE

WE'VE GOT STRATEGY COVERED

Prima
GAMES

primagames.com